The
Objective Guide
to Fixed and Indexed
Annuities

2201 East Grand River Avenue
Lansing, MI 48912-3296

BOOKS PUBLISHED BY QUANTUM PRESS

The
Objective Guide
to Fixed and Indexed
Annuities

ROBERT A. ESPERTI

RENNO L. PETERSON

PATRICK A. JEFFERS

Published for
The Masters Institute

——·A NOTE TO THE READER·——

The authors are not engaged in rendering legal, tax, investment, accounting, or similar professional services. While such legal, tax, accounting, and investment issues covered in this book have been verified with sources believed to be reliable, some material may be affected by changes in the laws or in the interpretations of such laws since the manuscript for this book was completed. For that reason, the accuracy and completeness of such information and the opinions based thereon are not guaranteed. In addition, state or local tax laws or procedural rules may have a material impact on the general conclusions made by the authors, and the judgments outlined in this book may not be suitable for every individual. For legal, tax, accounting, investment, or other similar issue expert advice is required by the professional services of competent practitioners. The authors are principals in TMI III, Inc., *The Masters Institute*, in pursuit of their vision to better fund America's estate plans; and receive compensation from it as a result of the compensation it receives from its Member advisors. The authors do not sell, distribute, or recommend carrier products to the public.

ISBN: 978-0-9850456-2-3

First Edition

Published for
The Masters Institute
by Quantum Press LLC

·DEDICATION·

To Our Masters Institute Colleagues

For the past three decades, we have mentored and collaborated with thousands of estate planning attorneys to change the way America plans by replacing bare-bones will-planning and probate with living trusts filled with meaningful instructions. Our bestselling book, *Loving Trust* (Viking-Penguin) and its Masters Institute update, *21st Century Loving Trust*, have been, and continue to be instrumental in accomplishing that goal.

Today, we are equally—if not more—committed to *helping America's families objectively and thoughtfully fund those plans to ensure the well-being of their loved ones and the fulfillment of their charitable desires.*

As we enlisted the aid of the nation's top estate planning attorneys to achieve our first goal, today we are working in collaboration with America's leading financial advisors as Fellows of our Masters Institute to accomplish our new goal.

We have labored over *The Objective Guide to Fixed and Indexed Annuities* and now share the methodologies we have developed with our Institute Fellows knowing that they will be instrumental in heightening planning awareness and professionalism in objectively funding America's retirement and estate plans.

We are grateful for their collegiality and encouragement, because this book is theirs as much as it is ours. A listing of these committed professionals and how they can be reached can be found in Appendix A.

·ACKNOWLEDGMENTS·

This book reflects the many contributions of annuity stalwarts whose volume of extraordinary work spans decades in influencing industry executives, actuaries, and many thousands of annuity advisors—all of whom have benefited greatly from their efforts.

We especially wish to acknowledge the following individuals for the scope and preciseness of their writings, and how helpful they have been to our research in seeking the truth about fixed and indexed annuities:

Jack Marrion

The "professor" and undisputed annuity "icon" whose body of scholarly work we professionally respect and deeply appreciate

John Olsen

Technical writer extraordinaire and enlightened advisor practitioner

Kim O'Brien

Pioneering consumer advocate and industry leader, whose enthusiasm and body of thoughtful work have made a good industry an even better industry

David Babbell

Professor of Insurance and Finance, Wharton School of Business and University of Pennsylvania; and Fellow of the Wharton Financial Institutions Center, for his academic prowess and objectivity

·CONTENTS·

Contents

·PREFACE·

To our dismay during recent years, it has become clear to us and to a great many of our advisor and attorney colleagues, that the retirement and estate plans of too many families are seriously deficient; not because of poor lawyering, but because families do not have the financial resources to achieve their planning goals.

Given our collective eighty years of experience as practitioners, mentors, and academicians, we have reflected on the source of this lack of funding, and have concluded that too many families' resources have been lost to the ongoing increases in living expenses or to losses attributed to the volatility of stock, bond, real estate, and commodity markets.

We undertook the writing of this book in tandem with our Masters Institute colleagues based on our collective commitment to help America's families better fund their retirement and estate plans.

Fixed and indexed annuities do not suffer market losses. However, they have their detractors. In seeking to understand whether these annuities can ensure improved retirement and estate funding results for America's families, we researched and reviewed the criticisms of annuity opponents, and the praises of annuity advocates, and subjected both to the critical analyses that we share with you in the chapters that follow.

To ensure the *Guide's* technical accuracy, we worked closely with an annuity expert, Patrick A. Jeffers—our Institute's Executive Director and our contributing author, who answered our every question, reviewed the body of our voluminous research, and checked every word in our manuscript to ensure its technical accuracy.

We hope you will appreciate the book's evenhandedness and candor, and that you will be able to use it to objectively determine if a fixed or indexed annuity is suitable to meet your specific retirement and estate planning goals.

Robert A. Esperti
Renno L. Peterson
July, 2014

———————

This *Guide* has been long overdue in the annuity marketplace! Much has been written about fixed and indexed annuities by many media pundits—both detractors and proponents—who have had little regard for the rigors of research and analysis, and the fairness and frankness found in this book.

I have been honored to participate in creating the *Guide* with Bob and Renno as my long-standing colleagues. In studying its commentary and the precision of its language, I know it to be the most accurate and understandable text yet written on fixed and indexed annuities. I believe it will be an invaluable tool in helping readers judge the suitability of fixed or indexed annuities to meet their retirement and estate planning objectives.

I am proud that The Masters Institute has sponsored its publication and to have been involved with Bob and Renno through all of the rigors of bringing it to completion.

Patrick A. Jeffers
July, 2014

·CHAPTER 1·

The Mechanics of Annuity Basics

Annuities have a language all their own—a jargon heavily laden with technical words, phrases, and acronyms that are unfamiliar and intimidating to most people.

Beginning with this chapter, we have done our best to stay away from the jargon as much as possible to give you a basic understanding and overview of what fixed and indexed annuities are all about and what they can do for you.

Our aversion to technical language will continue through each of the chapters that follow. In avoiding it, we mean no disrespect to our professional colleagues who habitually use and rely upon it to do their business. We avoid it only to increase our ability to give you a quicker and better understanding of the subject matter at hand.

❖ *What's a commercial annuity?*

A **commercial annuity** *(bold terms are found in the Guide's Glossary)* is a contract between you and a life insurance company, where you give the company money—usually in a lump sum—in exchange for the company's promise to give it back to you over a period of time with added interest or in some cases, appreciation in the value of the principal.

❖ *What's a private annuity?*

Private annuities are not the subject of this *Guide*. They are used in estate planning between family members for purposes other than saving money and receiving a guaranteed rate of return.

❖ *Are there different types of commercial annuities?*

Yes, and here is a quick overview of them:

- **Variable Annuities.** These are "investment vehicles" whose value goes up and down based upon stock market changes, and that do not contain guarantees. They are *not* the subject of this *Guide*.

- **Fixed Annuities.** These are "financial vehicles" that are guaranteed by the general funds of the life insurance companies offering them. They are also often referred to as **deferred annuities**, because their payouts occur for time periods that start years after they are purchased. This *Guide* is all about **fixed annuities**.

- **Indexed Annuities.** These are a unique hybrid-type of fixed annuity that combines the benefits of fixed annuity guarantees with some variable-like features to provide you with more upside in what your annuity might make. This Guide is also all about indexed annuities.

- **Single-Premium Immediate Annuities.** These annuities are not variable, fixed, or indexed. What distinguishes them is that rather than deferring payments, they immediately start periodic payments to you—usually within a month of your signing the contract and making a single deposit with the insurance company.

The fixed and indexed annuities referred to in this *Guide* are **deferred annuities** designed to give your money back to you on a guaranteed basis at a later time under whatever payment options you select.

❖ *Who are the parties to an annuity?*

Commercial annuities involve:

- *A life insurance company* that acts much like a bank in that it invests the money you give to it in their general fund to make a profit and then pays it back to you at a guaranteed interest or greater earnings rate.

- A *person* like you or your *IRA*—an annuity owner—who:

    1. wants to save and protect his or her principal by entering into a guaranteed annuity contract with the company; and

    2. determines what decisions need to be made about how the annuity contract is to be structured, and when and how payments are ultimately going to be received back from the insurance company.

- A *person*—also *you* (the textbooks refer to you here as an annuitant, but we promise not to)—whose life expectancy is used to determine the payments that will ultimately be made to your beneficiary if you elect to leave your money with the insurance company.

- And lastly, one or more *payees* who receive payments from the insurance company, most likely starting with you and thereafter *beneficiaries*, someone else you name (most usually, your spouse).

❖ In general, how does a life insurance company profit from fixed and indexed annuities?

They are betting that you will leave your money with them for an extended period during which they can invest it and make profits that will be greater than what they will ultimately give back to you; very much like how banks make money.

They are also betting that if you elect to leave your money with them for the rest of your life, you won't live to life expectancy; and you're betting that you will exceed it—by as long as you can.

Because insurance companies are very good at investing money, and people like you will leave your money with them for extended periods of time; and because not everyone will live as long as expected—annuities are big and profitable business.

❖ When do I start receiving my money back?

Before we answer, it's necessary to describe two separate periods during which the life insurance company does different things with your money:

- **Period One** is called the **accumulation period**, which is when the company uses your money to make money for itself by making investments in conservative bonds, and make money for you as well through your guaranteed income rate.

- **Period Two** is called the **annuitization period**, which is when the company starts paying your principal back to you, plus any earnings on it.

You decide when your annuity payments begin and the manner in which you want to receive them. To some extent, when these payments begin and the manner in which you receive them depends on the type of commercial annuity you purchase.

❖ But, when do I start receiving my money back?

During period one, you can take your money back any time, but if you take it back too soon, the company will charge you a penalty for your doing so—just like a bank charges you a penalty for cashing in a certificate of deposit early—based upon your contract's surrender charge schedule.

If you decide to take your money out after the expiration of the surrender charge schedule, you can do so without a penalty, just like a CD.

If you decide to leave your money with the insurance company and thereafter start Period Two, you will receive periodic principal and interest payments for a predetermined period or for the rest of your life, and perhaps continuing on for others thereafter.

❖ What's a fixed annuity?

A **fixed annuity** is a contract between you and the life insurance company in which you give the company money and it invests it in conservative bond investments. In return, the company promises to *guarantee the return of your principal* and to pay you a *guaranteed rate of interest.*

In fixed annuities, the company, on each anniversary date of your policy, upwardly adjusts your interest rate above its guaranteed rate—if rates go up—with what they call their **declared rate**.

In addition, the insurance company provides you with a number of different payment options that you can select that best fit your income needs when you elect to take money out of your annuity.

❖ *What are the major benefits that fixed annuities can provide for me?*

The *major* benefits of fixed annuities that most all the literature touts—whether in books, on the internet, through company promotional literature, or when advisors consult with people like you—are:

- Income-tax-deferred growth of your money that will maximize your annuity payments when you need them later for retirement

- A meaningful way to save, accumulate, and hold your principal intact

- A guaranteed interest rate to make your principal consistently grow over time

- A non-guaranteed, annually-adjusted company **declared interest rate** if it is greater—but not less than your guaranteed rate

- The company's *guarantee* that your money—principal and interest—will be there when you or your loved ones need it

❖ *In general, what's an indexed annuity?*

An **indexed annuity** is a variant of a fixed annuity and was invented in the mid-1990s. It can be likened to a cross between a fixed annuity and a variable annuity

Like a fixed annuity, it guarantees the return of your principal and a minimum rate of return. It also has a guaranteed percentage or amount that your principal can go up based on the performance of the stock markets, somewhat like a variable annuity but without the same investment risk.

❖ *How does the insurance company provide these guarantees and provide an upside based on the markets with an indexed annuity?*

The insurance company ties the growth of your money to the performance of the stock markets through various stock market indexes like Standard and Poor's, but protects your principal with guarantees

The result is that an indexed annuity gives you the possibility of making a greater return than your guaranteed rate. Your annuity receives a percentage of the upside in stock market performance, but is totally protected from market losses

In addition to these insurance company benefits, you may also receive an additional guaranteed minimum interest rate or "floor" that is typically a 1.5 percent rate on 87.5 percent of your deposit, less any withdrawals. This feature is often referred to as a "minimum interest guarantee" or the "non-forfeiture value" required by the National Association of Insurance Commissioners.

❖ *Are fixed and indexed annuities categorized as investments?*

The regulatory authorities agree that fixed and indexed annuities should never be categorized or referred to as investments. They are not subject to the complex federal regulations that govern variable annuities.

❖ *What if the markets go down?*

As we said, with an indexed annuity you cannot lose your money, because the insurance company guarantees your principal even if the equity markets and the indexes they track go down in any given number of years.

❖ *Are you saying that if the markets go up, my principal goes up, and if they go down my principal doesn't?*

Yes, that's what we are saying

However, you need to know the rest of the story. Your principal doesn't go up 100 percent with the various indexes it is tied to. It only goes up based upon a portion of the increase in the indexes, and does so depending upon a host of factors that you'll learn about in the following chapters.

❖ *Why can't my money go up 100 percent with the market indexes it's linked to?*

This is one way the insurance company makes money on the annuity. If you received all of the upside and none of the downside, it is likely that you would lose everything, because the insurance company would go bankrupt.

❖ *With all these guarantees, do I still have risk if the life insurance company goes out of business?*

You do, but as you will learn, insurance company failures are rare; and even rarer if attention is paid to the quality of their ratings by the professional rating services.

However, your concern is valid, and because ratings are so significant, we devote a chapter to them that focuses on what can cause an insurance company to fail, and what you need to look at in deciding what company to use.

❖ *What's the bottom-line of what indexed annuities can do for me?*

- Income-tax-deferred growth of your money that will maximize your annuity payments when you need them later for retirement.

- A meaningful way to accumulate and hold your principal.

- The opportunity to increase your principal if the equity market indexes go up in value greater than your contract's guaranteed rate.

- The company's guarantee that your money—principal and earnings—will be available when you or your loved ones need it.

Chapter Highlights

1. A commercial annuity is a contract with a life insurance company, in which you give the company money—usually in a lump sum—in exchange for the company's promise to give it back to you over a period of time with added interest or in some cases, any appreciation in value of the principal.

2. The "big three" annuity types are variable, fixed, and indexed.

3. Variable annuities are considered a publicly-traded security, such as a stock and bond, and subject to market risk; and are not the subject of this *Guide*.

4. In fixed annuities, a life insurance company promises to guarantee the return of your principal and pay you a guaranteed rate of interest.

5. Indexed annuities are like fixed annuities, except that the insurance company guarantees a maximum percentage or amount that your principal can go up based upon the performance of the stock market indexes, somewhat like a variable annuity, but without the same investment risks.

·CHAPTER 2·

Comparing Annuities to Bank Certificates of Deposit

The financial literature is filled with articles and charts comparing certificates of deposit (CDs) with fixed and indexed annuities. In our research, we have found that these articles often conflict with one another, especially when they use charts. Each chart generally lists the features common to both giving a simple "yes" or "no" rating next to each feature, followed by short comments summarizing the author's judgments.

For example, the "penalty-free withdrawals" feature is usually followed by "no" for CDs and "yes" next to annuities, but that's not the whole story. In fact, this "yes/no" categorization is vastly misleading across the board, because in most instances the "yes" or "no" requires a much more detailed explanation.

To provide you with a more complete explanation, the following pages compare the features common to CDs and annuities, along with our assessment of the objective differences between them.

❖ *Aren't CDs and fixed and indexed annuities investments?*

Articles that refer to them as investments are incorrect. They are not categorized by regulatory agencies as investments, and therefore are not regulated like publicly traded investments such as stocks and bonds.

❖ Does the length or term of each have importance?

Absolutely, and this is where CDs and annuities have major differences.

The short or long-term intent of the saver is initially determinative of whether annuities or CDs should be considered. Bank CDs are short-term savings vehicles that typically have time spans of one to five years. Annuities are generally long-term vehicles designed for periods well in excess of five years.

❖ Are the interest rates between them about the same?

There are many different methods for comparing the interest rates of CDs and annuities. The results often reflect the predisposition and bias of the pundit making the comparison and the particular methodology employed.

In our view, the preponderance of literature concludes that the rates for fixed annuities are generally higher than CDs by 1 to 2 percent. This means that if you have a CD earning 4 percent and an annuity earning 5 percent, the difference of 1 percent is a 25 percent increase over 4 percent; a significant return difference. If you couple that difference with the tax-deferred interest in an annuity, the difference is even greater.

❖ How can fixed annuity interest rates keep pace with or exceed CD bank rates?

Fixed annuities have a guaranteed rate just like CDs. In addition to the guaranteed rate, the insurance company that issues an annuity uses declared rates, and adjusts that rate upward or downward on the anniversary date of the annuity contract given the reality of current interest rates. These adjustments can never be lower than the rate guaranteed in the annuity contract.

By applying current rates, an annuity can keep pace with the short-term CD bank interest rates.

❖ *How do indexed annuity rates compare to CD interest rates?*

This question assumes an "apples to oranges" comparison because of the indexed feature of this type of annuity.

Indexed annuities have an upside earnings rate that is a percentage of the increase in the indexes they incorporate. See Chapter 5, How Your Money Grows inside Your Indexed Annuity, for more detail on this important subject.

In addition, the National Association of Insurance Commissioners (NAIC) mandates that indexed annuities provide an additional guaranteed minimum interest rate ("floor") that is typically a 1.5 percent rate on 87.5 percent of your money, less any withdrawals. This required feature is often referred in industry jargon as a "minimum interest guarantee" or the "non-forfeiture value."

❖ *Do CDs, fixed annuities, and indexed annuities act equally well as hedges against inflation?*

CDs and fixed annuities are not touted by financial experts as hedges against inflation.

Advocates of indexed annuities properly argue that they provide a limited inflation hedge, because insurance companies credit earnings against increases in the indexes which the annuity is based on.

To create a true hedge against inflation, a new fixed annuity variant has been created called an **inflation-protected annuity** or **inflation-indexed annuity**. These annuities guarantee a rate of return that is equal to or greater than the rate of inflation, similar to the annual cost-of-living adjustment (COLA) feature in Social Security. However, in terms of practicality, these vehicles currently are not offered by many companies, and their cost may be too prohibitive for many consumers.

❖ Are CDs and fixed and indexed annuities equally safe as to the protection of principal?

CDs are guaranteed by the Federal Deposit Insurance Corporation (FDIC) up to $250,000 per account.

Fixed and indexed annuities are guaranteed by the life insurance companies issuing them. They are also guaranteed by state guarantee funds. State guarantees range from a low of $100,000 to a high of $500,000, with many in the $250,000 range.

You can easily find your state's guarantee amount by doing an Internet search for State Annuity Guide. Click on the link to this guide and a map will appear on your screen that allows you to click on your state to ascertain the amount of its guarantee. (If you have trouble finding this guide, the actual URL for the map is: http://www.findyourannuity.com/Annuities/State-Annuity-Guide.)

❖ Are these state guarantees well-known and discussed by advisors?

They are.

❖ Isn't the FDIC guarantee for CDs stronger?

Of course, there is no question that the U.S. government's guarantee is far stronger than any life insurance company guarantee.

Those who favor annuities and their company-backed guarantees point to how few life insurance company failures have occurred compared to the much larger number of bank failures during the same time periods, and how safe you are with quality companies that have the highest ratings.

What doesn't make sense to us is that regardless of how many additional bank failures there are, if you keep your account to less than $250,000, the number of bank failures simply doesn't matter; your money will still be protected by the FDIC.

We did a significant amount of research in this area, and found that it is true that insurance company failures are relatively minor and relatively non-existent compared to bank failures. It is also true that with a few exceptions, companies that did fail *did not* have top ratings, but rather abysmally low ones. We also found a couple of exceptions where the insurance company was highly rated and failed.

To be fair, it should be noted that life insurance companies today are more closely regulated than in the past; and are required to invest their assets conservatively, mostly in long-term bonds. They are required to maintain capital equal to their policy commitments on pretty much a dollar-to-dollar basis.

This is a very important topic and we have devoted a chapter to it. See Chapter 3, How Good Are Life Insurance Company Guarantees?

❖ *Can I use multiple annuities to stay within a state's maximums for each one, like having multiple CDs with different account names to get maximum FDIC coverage on each?*

Unfortunately, you cannot. The statutes we've reviewed are written for total aggregation per person.

❖ Are the income tax attributes of fixed and indexed annuities better than the income taxation of CDs?

This is the major feature that annuity enthusiasts ascribe to the superiority of annuities over CDs, and they are totally correct! If you own an annuity outside of your IRA, it compounds interest on a tax-deferred basis. If you own a CD outside of your IRA, it does *not* receive this same tax benefit.

If your annuity or your CDs are owned by your IRA, they both compound on a tax-deferred basis, so that the deferral added by your annuity is redundant and provides no additional income tax benefit.

❖ Do fixed and indexed annuities and CDs offer flexibility in terms of their planning options?

The comparisons between CDs and fixed annuities generally do not address the issue of flexibility.

Fixed and indexed annuities have been accurately categorized as more flexible than CDs, because of the many options that are available under the riders that can be purchased as part of these contracts—options that do not exist with CDs.

However, CD proponents can rightly point out that their shorter terms create far more flexibility.

❖ Do fixed and indexed annuities have better withdrawal rights than CDs?

There are usually penalties for early withdrawals from CDs, even if the withdrawal is one day prior to maturity.

In comparing penalties, those who favor annuities sometimes lead the reader to conclude that annuities are free of early-withdrawal penalties, which is an over-generalization and, depending upon how it is stated, an exaggeration. With annuities, you can only receive early annuity distributions free of penalty under the terms of the surrender charge schedule in your annuity contract. These schedules reduce the penalty for early withdrawals by a reducing percentage by year until there is no charge at the end of the schedule (usually five, seven, or ten years).

In fairness, most company annuity schedules allow a 10 percent penalty-free withdrawal at the beginning of their surrender charge schedules, which likely leads to their "superior" claims of their advocates.

Given the objective facts, annuities do get the nod over CDs in this area with their early-withdrawal features and schedules allowing withdrawals over time.

❖ What does a typical surrender charge schedule look like?

A typical surrender charge schedule might read something like this:

> *The full annuity value of your contract is available to you without any surrender charges after the contract has been in force for ten full contract years. (Withdrawals prior to age 59½ may be subject to a 10% tax penalty and withdrawals are subject to ordinary income tax.) If you need to surrender your contract prior to the end of ten years, you can do so subject to a surrender charge as shown in this schedule:*

Contract Year:	1	2	3	4	5	6	7	8	9	10	11+
Surrender Charge (%)	10	9	8	7	6	5	4	3	2	1	0

❖ Are CDs and fixed and indexed annuities equally liquid?

For the most part, CDs are shorter term than annuities and because of their shorter terms, can claim the edge on liquidity.

On the other hand, fixed and indexed annuities have early-withdrawal rights and penalty-free withdrawal provisions, regardless of whether the annuity is for five, seven, or ten years; so perhaps they do have a valid liquidity claim.

In our view, given the different terms for their use, comparisons cannot be reasonably and objectively made.

❖ Do CDs, fixed annuities, and indexed annuities avoid probate?

Annuity advocates who claim that annuity proceeds avoid probate are correct: Annuities have a named beneficiary, so probate is not necessary. Their claims that CDs do not, are not totally correct.

If CDs are held in joint tenancy, in a living trust, or have payable-on-death provisions, they will avoid probate. If they don't fall under these usual planning devices, they will become probate assets.

❖ Are annuity buyers subject to large commissions that banks don't charge for issuing CDs?

Annuity proponents argue that you *do not* pay commissions and front-end fees when purchasing an annuity.

Annuity opponents take the opposite position, because life insurance companies do pay advisors commissions on the sale of annuities.

Given the notoriety and sensitivity of this issue, we have extensively researched the arguments on both sides, and shake our heads as to the position of the annuity opponents.

In our view, their negative allegations are ill-founded and relatively baseless:

- Yes; life insurance companies pay commissions on annuities—just like every for-profit company pays its salespeople or distributers to sell its goods or services.

- But, *you do not pay* a direct sales commission when you purchase an annuity.

- The cost of delivery is built into the overall cost and performance of the annuity contract, just like the cost of a CD is built into its rate. The costs of delivering any good or service is built into its pricing as well, including our legal and consulting fees over the years, or the royalties we receive for writing books.

Set-up charges fall within the same reasoning. They are built into the annuity contract as a life insurance company's cost of doing business.

Given the importance of this area to annuity critics, we devote Chapter 10, Commissions and Fees, to a discussion and analysis of the issue.

❖ *Are CDs and fixed and indexed annuities protected from the claims of creditors?*

Annuity advocates claim that an annuity's protection from creditors is one of its major virtues as compared to CDs.

In the main, they are correct. In comparing the two, it is clear that CDs are fully subject to the claims of their owners' creditors. However, when it comes to annuities, the answers are not so clear.

As estate planning attorneys, the temptation to truly delve into this feature is great, but not appropriate for this *Guide*. So with disciplined difficulty, we limit our commentary here on this very important planning subject.

In short, the universal claim by annuity protagonists that annuities are free from creditor claims is totally correct in some cases; partially right in others; and totally wrong in yet others.

Here is a summary of the law on the subject:

- First, the Federal Bankruptcy Act's exemption for the right to receive payments under an annuity is not particularly generous, and not heavily relied upon by creditor planning attorneys for protecting the assets of their clients.

- Second, the laws of each state determine if, and to what degree, annuity funds are subject to the claims of creditors.

- Third, in some states, annuities are exempt from creditors; in others they are not exempt at all. In the majority of states, they are exempt under certain situations, and subject to a variety of terms and maximums as defined in each state's statutes. These statutes are all over the board as to their protections.

If your state's statutes are of interest to you, it's relatively easy to perform an Internet search to read the law as it applies to you or, better yet, ask your advisor to do so for you.

❖ Can additional contributions be made to both fixed annuities and CDs?

The easy answer is yes for annuities, and no for CDs. In reality you can always purchase another CD as long as you can meet the bank's minimum amount requirement for doing so.

❖ **Is the principal placed in CDs and fixed annuities free of market fluctuations?**

The answer is yes for CDs and fixed annuities. Indexed annuities are subject to market fluctuations in up markets, but not in down ones.

❖ **Do CDs have a guaranteed lifetime income option like annuities?**

They do not.

❖ **Are CD earnings and annuity earnings both excluded from Social Security tax calculations?**

Annuity earnings are *excluded*, while CD earnings are *included* in Social Security tax calculations.

Chapter Highlights

1. Do not rely on basic charts or articles when comparing annuities and CDs; they are often gross generalizations or incorrect.

2. Annuities owned outside of IRAs compound interest on a tax-deferred basis, giving them a significant advantage over CDs that are owned outside of IRAs.

3. Annuities will generally pay a greater rate of return than CDs, because of the features they contain and their ability to defer income taxes.

4. CDs are protected by the FDIC. Annuities are protected by life insurance company guarantees; and some states have additional protections for annuities.

5. Both CDs and annuities are subject to delivery and distribution costs and related expenses, so it is incorrect to state that CDs do not have sales commissions and annuities do.

6. Both CDs and annuities have penalties for early withdrawals, but annuities have exceptions to penalties that allow annuity owners to withdraw certain amounts at certain times without penalty.

·CHAPTER 3·

How Good Are Life Insurance Company Guarantees?

This topic is highly controversial in the literature and among our colleagues, because fixed and indexed annuity purchasers like you rely on the guarantees of life insurance companies when purchasing fixed and indexed annuities.

Annuity proponents argue with fervor that fixed and indexed annuities are among the safest and most conservative places you can put your money. They are adamant that quality life insurance companies—those that are rated most highly by commercial rating services—are rock-solid in buttressing their annuity-based guarantees.

Annuity antagonists argue with equal passion that life insurance companies are not to be trusted; that they go broke just like other businesses, and in fact have a track record of doing so.

Deciphering facts and discovering the truth is not easy on this issue, but, in the questions and answers that follow, we will do our best to give you the facts as objectively as we can.

❖ *What are the criticisms that annuity antagonists levy against what they characterize as the "phoniness" of life insurance company guarantees?*

Their criticisms can be summarized as follows:

- Life insurance companies can go broke, and have a history of doing so; to place your savings with them is risky business and unnecessary.

- A great many annuity "sellers" are recommending and writing annuities with companies that are not financially solid, and therefore unsafe.

❖ *Okay, so life Insurance companies have failed. Have they failed more or less than banks?*

Yes; life insurance companies have failed, but they have failed far less than banks.

We covered this comparison between bank failures and life insurance company failures in chapter 2.

In our judgment, however, the number of bank failures, as numerous as they may be in comparison to life insurance company failures, is simply immaterial in the comparison used by annuity supporters.

Regardless of whether or not your bank fails, if you take proper precautions in setting up your accounts, you won't you lose your money, because of the Federal Deposit Insurance Corporation (FDIC).

❖ *How many life insurance companies have failed in the past thirty years?*

In the early 1990s, three major companies went under: Mutual Benefit Life Insurance Company, Confederation Life Insurance Company, and Executive Life Insurance Company. They all failed because of illiquid asset concentrations that led to a failure to meet maturing obligations.

❖ Why do you qualify your answer to the previous question with "major" life insurance companies?

We did so because most professional annuity advisors and knowledgeable clients would never consider buying annuities from a weak, small, or new and unproven company that lacked a history of stability and proven resources (management and capital); and that did not have the *highest ratings* from recognized rating agencies. The insurance companies that failed have been almost exclusively poorly rated companies.

❖ What do you mean by "highest ratings"?

Life insurance companies are rated by independent commercial rating agencies. These are companies that specialize in assessing the creditworthiness of life insurance companies and give them a grade very much like you were graded during your school years (A, A−, B+, etc.)

Your professional advisor will refer to these ratings in recommending one or more companies to you. We discuss them and what they mean toward the end of this chapter.

❖ Did Mutual Benefit's annuity holders lose money when the company went under?

That's a really good question, because Mutual Benefit was founded in 1845, and was the biggest insurance company failure in United States history. It had billions in obligations to 285,000 holders of individual life insurance policies and annuities when it went under.

After it declared insolvency, the New Jersey Department of Insurance engineered a court-approved plan for "rehabilitation"— in short, the company was taken over by a healthy subsidiary, and the policyholders were paid first. They were paid during the recovery period, and their payments included their guaranteed interest. Bottom-line, they did not lose any money in the annuities they had with Mutual Benefit.

❖ Did Confederation Life policyholders lose money?

Confederation Life was a large and venerable Canadian company founded in 1871 that was doing considerable business in the United States.

In its case, within one week of its declared insolvency, the Canadian Policyholder Guaranty Organization, a government oversight agency, called for cash funding contributions by the other Canadian insurers, and policyholders were protected.

The story doesn't end there. Creditors sued, claiming they were due money first, but they lost their case. In an 87-page opinion, the Canadian court concluded: "The claimants have claims against the estate of Confederation Life Insurance Company. They are claims, however, as ordinary creditors or, at least, claims which *rank behind those of Confederation Life's policyholders.*" (emphasis added)

❖ Did Executive Life's policyholders lose money?

They did!

But, let's start their story with the end in mind, because the saga of Executive Life is truly a unique and sordid tale; like something right out of Hollywood—which it was.

Here's the end of the story, according to Jack Marrion, a much-respected annuity industry scholar and expert: "Everyone who did not surrender their Executive Life annuity eventually got back at least their principal and contractually guaranteed interest."[1]

In researching this case, we agree with his conclusion; however, the background prior to the end is not pretty. It was neatly summarized by a November, 2008 *New York Times* article:

> "[A]t the time of its demise in 1991, it had about two-thirds of its assets invested in junk bonds (Mr. Milken's company sold them, and Executive Life's parent company eagerly took them in).
>
> "When the value of those bonds fell, many policyholders took their business elsewhere, in an insurance version of a run on the bank. California's insurance commissioner seized the company's unit in that state, a move regulators elsewhere quickly copied.
>
> "While Executive Life continued to pay out claims when people died, other policyholders who stayed with the company were not allowed to cash in their policies or borrow against them except in case of hardship. Some types of monthly annuity payments dropped to 70 percent of what they were supposed to be.
>
> "The measures were supposed to be temporary, but the stopgap ended up lasting for two and a half years."

So, those who cashed out early lost money. Those who did not do so eventually got their money back.

❖ *Aren't you troubled by the Executive Life case?*

We certainly are. We are particularly concerned, because Executive Life was a major company that was highly rated by the rating agencies immediately prior to its going under.

That being said, there are three factors that lead us to believe that our apprehension is not necessarily warranted.

1. The other cases we've researched show substantially different results, leading us to conclude that Executive Life was an aberration.

2. Since Executive Life failed, the rating agencies have substantially increased their vigilance.

3. The National Association of Insurance Commissioners has taken a much stronger role in regulating insurance companies through the fifty states' insurance commissioners.

However, we still recommend caution. We have always told our clients: *To plan for the best is not planning—it's wishful thinking. Always plan for the worst, so you won't be unpleasantly surprised.*

We don't think it wise for you to purchase a fixed or indexed annuity from any carrier that is not highly rated by the rating agencies—*period*. We will cover ratings in the pages that follow.

❖ *What happened to life insurance companies during the Great Recession?*

To quote a Standard and Poor's "white paper" on this very important subject:

> "Perhaps, surprisingly, the global financial crisis that began in 2007 failed to trigger a wave of life [insurance] defaults among rated companies. In fact, not one significant [life insurance company] that Standard and Poor's rated at that time…has defaulted due to the financial crisis."

❖ *Haven't there been other companies that have gotten into trouble during the past thirty years that you didn't mention?*

Yes, there have. In the adjustable rate mortgage debacle in 1995, the General American Life Insurance Company was taken over by the Missouri Department of Insurance, but it was acquired by Metropolitan Life one week later, and the policyholders were totally protected.

❖ *Are these stories truly an accurate portrayal of what happens to life insurance companies that get into trouble?*

They are. State insurance commissions immediately get involved in these situations and work quickly to protect policyholders.

❖ *Wouldn't AIG have gone under if the federal government hadn't bailed it out?*

Another respected industry luminary, Joe Tomlinson, deftly summarized this incredibly tangled and complicated situation:

> "AIG stands out as the poster child for making advisors and the public nervous about insurance companies.
>
> "This was an AAA− rated company that, almost overnight, found itself in need of a $182 billion bailout from the [f]ederal government. The natural question for prospective annuity investors to ask is: 'What would have happened to AIG annuity owners if the federal government had not stepped in?'
>
> "AIG was (and remains) a diversified financial conglomerate, and the huge losses from credit default swaps were

concentrated in its financial products division. The insurance subsidiaries of AIG that sold annuities remained reasonably healthy during the crisis. The losses befell a separate legal entity, which means that creditors seeking restitution…could not have laid claim to insurance subsidiary assets. If AIG had tried to move assets out of the insurance subsidiaries, insurance commissioners in the various states would have blocked such attempts. *So while AIG set off huge alarms in the financial system, it was not a crisis for their basic life insurance and annuity business.*(emphasis added)"[2]

❖ *Given all these "good" ending stories, are you suggesting that I don't have to worry about the creditworthiness of a life insurance company when buying a fixed or indexed annuity?*

Absolutely not!

We have only tried to objectively respond to the accusations, attacks, and criticisms of annuity antagonists that: (1) "the guarantees of life insurance companies are not to be trusted;" and (2) "you should not put your money into a fixed or indexed annuity, because by doing so, you are taking a significant risk."

Based on our research, we are convinced that for you to place your savings with any company that doesn't have an "A" somewhere in its rating would be foolhardy. Doing so would be taking an unnecessary risk that you do not have to take. Put your money with top echelon, strong companies rather than their financially weaker competitors.

❖ *So, you are adamant that I should be concerned about the creditworthiness and strength of the company I place my business with.*

We are, and would like to address questions about the whole business of life insurance company ratings and the agencies that rate them.

❖ *How many life insurance rating agencies are there?*

For most annuity experts, there are only four that matter; along with a fifth one that rates an insurance company based on the combined ratings of the other four.

❖ *Who are they?*

In alphabetical order, the big four in the rating business are: A.M. Best, Fitch, Moody's, and Standard and Poor's. The fifth company, COMDEX, takes the ratings of the big four, averages them, and comes out with its own ratings.

❖ *Are they all the same, or is there one that is better than the others?*

There is no doubt that A.M. Best has been viewed over time as the "gold standard" in the business.

However, our research makes clear that before making a decision on what company to do business with, you should ask your advisor for the ratings of it by each of the four review companies—and ask for a COMDEX rating as well.

❖ *What makes A.M. Best so special?*

They've been in business since the San Francisco fire in 1906; and unlike the other three who rate all kinds of different industries, they focus and specialize exclusively in assessing companies in the insurance industry.

A.M. Best issues solid and relied-upon financial-strength ratings measuring insurance companies' ability to pay claims.

❖ *Specifically, what do they do?*

Best's "Financial Strength Ratings" represent its assessment of an insurer's ability to meet its obligations to policyholders. The rating process involves quantitative and qualitative reviews of a company's balance sheet, operating performance, and business profile, including comparisons to peers and industry standards and assessments of an insurer's operating plans, philosophy, and management. The rating formulas are proprietary.

Their rating scale includes six "secure" ratings.

❖ *What are their ratings?*

The first six are:

Rating	Description
A++	Superior
A+	Superior
A	Excellent
A−	Excellent
B++	Good
B+	Good

❖ *What about the rest of the ratings?*

In our view, they are unimportant because of what we acknowledge as our objective purpose and conservative bias: the security of your money.

If you are as concerned about preserving your money as we are for you to do so, you will never—ever—consider any rating other than one with an "A" in it.

❖ *If I can review the ratings of all four rating agencies, why would I need a COMDEX rating?*

It solves the difficulty of your having to interpret the different rating scales issued by the agencies. Each agency uses a different rating system and scale, which makes it difficult to compare the ratings of each, one to the other, to come up with a meaningful conclusion.

❖ *Is it really that difficult to review the ratings of the four rating agencies?*

It is. Here is an illustration of what we are trying to convey:

Suppose an insurance company has an AA rating from Agency 1 and an A+ rating from Agency 2. And, suppose the AA rating corresponds to the 90th percentile of the companies rated by Agency 1, that is, only 10 percent of the companies have a higher rating; and the A+ rating corresponds to the 80th percentile of the companies rated by Agency 2, that is, only 20 percent of the companies have a higher rating. The Comdex would be 85, the average of 90 and 80.[3]

❖ *How does COMDEX provide a "user friendly" rating?*

It reviews the ratings of all four agencies and averages them into a single numerical score that ranges from 1-100 with 100 being the highest rating possible.

❖ *What COMDEX number should I look for to be comfortable with?*

In interviewing a number of our colleagues, the consensus is a score of 75 or higher. However, this number is a threshold. Most large financial companies in the securities markets require a minimum of a 75 to 80 COMDEX rating. It is an acknowledged industry standard.

❖ *How many companies qualify for this number?*

We checked the COMDEX ratings as we were writing this. Out of 618 life insurance companies, 186 (30 percent) of them had a score of 75 or better.

❖ *Wouldn't it be easier to just get the COMDEX number and not worry about the ratings of the other four?*

In the view of knowledgeable industry experts, you would be making a grave mistake.

The COMDEX number is an average of the four. This methodology has a flaw in it. For example, three of the agencies could give a company the very highest ratings, and a fourth could give it an abysmal rating. The average might be high, but would ignore the *red flag* concerns of the fourth company.

In short, the issue quickly becomes, "What does the fourth rating agency know that the others don't?"

❖ *Given this flaw in the averaging system, wouldn't it be wise to get the COMDEX number and also look at the ratings of the other four?*

Precisely! And, our advice would be to look for an "A" somewhere in each of the other four's ratings, along with the all-important threshold of 75 to 80 or better COMDEX number.

❖ *Where can I get these ratings?*

Your advisor will provide them to you, because he or she will subscribe to all of the services, and can quickly ascertain what you need to know on an up-to-date basis about each company you may be considering.

❖ *Okay, here's a **really important** question. Do all annuity advisors and their clients pay attention to these ratings?*

Our research provides a really embarrassing answer: apparently they don't. *Two of the most popular life insurance companies who regularly record industry-leading sales in indexed annuities each have a COMDEX rating of 46 as we write this!*

❖ *What companies are they?*

It would be best for you to ask your annuity advisor this question, because COMDEX and other ratings frequently change.

❖ *That's unbelievable! Are you absolutely certain?*

We are; and it is because of situations like this that we were encouraged to research and write this *Guide* in conjunction with our Masters Institute colleagues to improve the way America funds its retirement and estate plans.

❖ *How is it possible that these companies can be rated so poorly and yet be industry-leading sellers?*

This is where the antagonists' criticisms have real teeth. Companies like these offer higher selling commissions, coupled with expanded promises to pay higher than market rates, and provide additional costly features that they are not properly charging for, as compared to safer and more financially prudent companies.

The allure of aggressive payments, bonuses, and interest rates makes people forget that *the single most important reason to purchase an annuity is to reduce the risk of losing their money.*

❖ Are most annuity advisors trustworthy?

In our view, they are. We believe that the majority of those who are selling inferior companies do so more out of ignorance than greed.

❖ But, if most life insurance companies don't go out of business, why shouldn't I buy an annuity that pays me a little more from a lesser-rated company?

While it's true that most companies don't go out of business, obviously there's always a risk with a lower rated company. So, why would you risk what you can't afford to lose, and possibly subject yourself to the travails of receivership just for a slightly better return? In our view, the risk/reward ratio for doing so wouldn't make sense.

❖ Should I still be concerned?

When it comes to protecting your money, you should always be concerned.

Armed with the knowledge you will gain from this *Guide*, and the advice and counsel of an annuity professional you trust, you should be able to rest easy with the decisions that you ultimately make.

Chapter Highlights

1. You should be concerned about the guarantees offered by the life insurance company that you are considering when purchasing a fixed or indexed annuity.

2. Life insurance companies have failed in the past, but those who purchased annuities almost always received their money back.

3. Only purchase annuities from companies that have at a minimum an A− rating from the top four rating companies, and a 75 or above rating from COMDEX.

4. Make sure your annuity professional shares all of the rating information with you.

·CHAPTER 4·

Do I Need Guaranteed Income
Now? Later? For Others? Never?

In order to determine your income needs, you must discuss a number of issues with your annuity advisor so that with his or her help, you can design one or more annuities to meet the specifics of your needs.

The options that are available to you in how you wish to receive your annuity payments are many. They are not complex, and are relatively straightforward.

The task before you is for you to consider and determine how you wish the payments from your annuity to be received.

For most people this has not been difficult, because they have a firm grasp of their fears and goals when it comes to financial security, and the income streams that they believe they, and perhaps their spouses, will need in the future as they mature and retire.

If, however, you do not have the ability to easily select from among the options that we discuss in this chapter, we would encourage you to seek the advice and counsel of an annuity professional you trust to discuss your quandaries.

❖ *Okay, what are the issues I should be considering in the initial design of my annuity?*

You need to discuss with your annuity advisor whether you want to:

- Start receiving annuity payments at once.

- Receive systematic withdrawals at intervals you select while you are still putting money into your annuity.

- Use your annuity to guarantee income only for your life and ending on your death.

- Receive an income for your life, but if you die before you receive all the money you put into your annuity, have your beneficiary receive regular payments; until the total of what the beneficiary receives, when added to what you received, equals the total amount of money you put in the annuity.

- Augment your income with additional payments at a future date.

- Provide guaranteed income for your retirement and, after your death, provide guaranteed income then for your spouse's lifetime.

- Forego payments to yourself in order to provide more significant guaranteed income for your spouse after your death.

- Pass your annuity proceeds to a beneficiary other than your spouse.

❖ *That's a lot of options! Does the life insurance company charge me differently for them?*

It does. Because each payment option contains a different risk to the company and provides a different benefit to you, the options are priced separately by the company's internal actuaries whose business is assessing risk, and assigning the right value and cost to each.

❖ *Where do I select the option or options I want?*

All options are found in the annuity application. Your advisor will help you fill it out to meet your particular needs.

❖ *How does the insurance company invest my money to perform on all of these options?*

According to the National Association of Insurance Commissioners (the commissioners of each state's insurance department): "Insurance companies invest the money you pay in bonds and mortgages with fixed rates of return. By doing so, you are guaranteed at least a specified minimum amount in each annuity payout period."

❖ *Is it important for me to forecast when I might need to start distributions from my annuity?*

Absolutely; forecasting will allow your advisor to design an annuity plan that meets your needs while minimizing unnecessary surrender charges.

❖ *What if I want to put a single sum of money in an annuity and immediately start taking distributions?*

You would do so by purchasing a **single-premium immediate annuity**, called a **SPIA** by industry professionals. It is a type of annuity that begins providing payouts immediately.

❖ *Why wouldn't I purchase a fixed or indexed annuity if I want to take income immediately?*

A fixed or indexed annuity would not be appropriate for you, because each is a deferred annuity that builds value during an accumulation period. Distributions begin when you elect to annuitize the annuity contract.

❖ ***What should be my primary consideration in considering the purchase of a fixed or indexed annuity?***

Your primary consideration should be projecting when you will need to begin taking annuity distributions for your retirement, or additional income to supplement your income.

❖ ***Can I elect to receive automatic distributions at specific times during my lifetime before the life insurance company annuitizes my money?***

You certainly can by choosing to take **systematic withdrawals**. They allow you to access your money during the accumulation period.

❖ ***What are the ways I can take my money out with systematic withdrawals?***

You can elect to receive your money in: (1) substantially equal payments over a specified period; (2) a specified dollar amount; or (3) a specified percentage of your account balance.

❖ ***If I elect to make systematic withdrawals, will I eventually reduce my annuity balance down to zero?***

Yes, unless you have an early death. Also, if you take distributions before you are 59½ years old, there is a 10 percent federal income tax penalty on any interest income that is distributed to you. This penalty is in addition to any income tax that is due.

❖ ***What if I don't elect to take systematic withdrawals?***

You'll elect to take another type of payment when you fill out the application with your advisor.

❖ **Can I purchase a fixed or indexed annuity that makes payments just to me at a later date?**

You can, it's called a **life-only annuity.** With a life-only annuity, you elect to annuitize your contract so that it will pay you income for as long as you live—regardless of your longevity. On your death the insurance company makes no further payments. This annuity pays you the highest income possible.

❖ **How does a life-only annuity differ from a SPIA?**

With a SPIA you receive immediate payouts. A life-only annuity allows you to defer payouts to a later time.

❖ **How can I plan for annuity payments during my lifetime and then for my spouse's lifetime?**

You can purchase a "last-survivor option" that pays income for both your life and that of your spouse. With this option, you have the flexibility to receive larger payments while you are both living, followed by lower payments after the first one of you dies.

❖ **What if my spouse predeceases me?**

You would continue to receive payments until your death.

❖ **Can I purchase a fixed or indexed annuity that will guarantee payments to me during my lifetime, and then for a specific number of years to my spouse?**

You can with a **life annuity with a period-certain** option. It will enable you to receive income for as long as you live, with the additional guarantee that the life insurance company will continue making regular payouts to your spouse—or any other beneficiary you choose—for a specified period of years, that typically ranges from five to twenty years.

❖ *Can I purchase a fixed or indexed annuity that names one or more beneficiaries after my death?*

You can.

❖ *Why would anyone put money in an annuity, and never plan to take it out during his or her lifetime?*

This often happens with married couples who are approaching or are over the age of retirement, where the breadwinner spouse wants to continue to save with a tax-deferred annuity. This strategy guarantees that the annuity principal will be available to the surviving spouse to supplement his or her income needs after the first spouse's death.

❖ *But, couldn't I do the very same thing with CDs or other investments?*

You could, but by placing them in a fixed or indexed annuity you will be able to grow them on an income-tax-deferred basis, while guaranteeing the preservation of your principal. See Chapter 2, Comparing Annuities to Bank Certificates of Deposit.

❖ *Can I take money out of my annuity in a single lump-sum distribution?*

You can withdraw all your money in a single payout. However, you must be mindful of the potential of a 10 percent early withdrawal penalty for federal income tax purposes on the interest it has earned if you are not yet 59½ years old, in addition to any income tax due on the interest. You also might have to pay a surrender charge fee to the insurance company.

❖ What if I don't take money out of my annuity during my lifetime?

In lieu of other options you may have selected, you would select a payment option providing that the proceeds go to your named beneficiaries; unless it's a life-only annuity, in which case there would be no proceeds.

❖ If I want to supplement my income on retirement or my spouse's income after I am gone, would I be better off with a fixed annuity or an indexed one?

If you don't believe that the equity markets will go up in the years to come, you would likely be more comfortable with a fixed annuity.

If you are concerned about inflation, and think that the current trend of steadily rising prices and stock values will continue, you would probably be more comfortable with an indexed annuity.

❖ Would I be wise to allocate a portion of my money to a fixed annuity, and the balance to an indexed one?

If you want to hedge your bet, it would be reasonable for you to combine a fixed annuity with an indexed one, allocating your dollars between them on whatever ratio you are most comfortable with.

Another alternative is to choose an option in your contract to allocate whatever percentage you want of your indexed annuity to a one-year fixed guaranteed rate that is referred to as a **fixed bucket**. Typically, you can do this every year on your anniversary date, and change the allocation however you would like.

❖ *Do all companies give me the right to do this?*

Most of them do, but not all. If a fixed-bucket option appeals to you, be sure to bring it to the attention of your advisor.

❖ *Can I buy an annuity without naming a beneficiary?*

You can if it is for your lifetime only. If it has survivorship features, however, you must name a beneficiary.

❖ *What is the most important issue you believe I should consider in forecasting the accumulation period for my annuity?*

The most important issue you should consider is the possibility that you will need all or part of your money earlier than your projections. Always consider the worst-case problems that could arise in your situation, and design your annuity planning accordingly.

❖ *Why is this worst-case thinking important in configuring my annuity?*

Surrender charge periods in annuities vary. You will probably have to pay an additional amount for a shorter surrender charge period, but it may be warranted in a particular situation.

Chapter Highlights

1. Knowing who you want to receive your annuity proceeds, and when those needs have to be met are essential factors in choosing the right annuity for you.

2. There are a number of annuity options, and each option is priced differently. Life insurance companies assess the risk and cost associated with each option to determine its price.

3. A fixed annuity has a guaranteed income amount; an indexed annuity is tied to stock market indexes, but still offers guaranteed amounts.

4. Surrender charges and income tax considerations may also affect the type of annuity or annuities that you choose.

·CHAPTER 5·

How Your Money Grows Inside Your Indexed Annuity

An apt metaphor for starting our chapter's discussion would be to compare an indexed annuity to the car you drive.

Do you know the details in your owner's manual? Can you go farther in your understanding, and grasp how the mechanical and electrical systems work together to make your car run?

If you are like most people, you will answer "no" to our questions, because although you know what your car can do for you, and understand perfectly well how to drive it, you have little knowledge about what actually makes it work.

The information in this chapter is just a little bit about how your annuity structurally works to produce desired results for both you and the insurance company you select.

Hopefully, after reading it you will be better prepared to make more informed decisions about the suitability of your annuity's structure, and to engage in more meaningful conversations with your annuity advisor.

❖ *Does the insurance company invest indexed annuity funds in stocks?*

No, the life insurance company does not buy shares of stock; it links your annuity to increases in the performance of whatever index or combination of indexes you select.

49

❖ *What do you mean by "linked"?*

If your index choice goes up in value, you get what is called **index interest**, which is a percentage of the index's increase in value. The amount of the index interest is automatically added to your annuity at the end of whatever time period you select.

❖ *What if the index goes down in value?*

Your annuity does not go down; that is part of the guarantee.

❖ *Typically, what indexes have been selected by people like me?*

The Standard and Poor's 500 Index.

❖ *How many different indexes are there for me to select from?*

As we write this, we counted 24 indexes among which you can make your choices.

❖ *Are companies adding additional indexes?*

Yes, they add them all the time.

❖ *Can I select more than one index?*

You can; and may allocate on a percentage basis among them.

❖ *How often can I change indexes and my allocations among them?*

Generally, you can do so on your annuity's anniversary date.

❖ *How important is my selection of indexes in determining what my annuity ultimately earns?*

In our view, it doesn't much matter what indexes you choose, because the results will generally be about the same.

❖ *Why doesn't my index selection meaningfully influence the extent of my annuity's earnings?*

As you will soon read, insurance companies need to limit the upside of what you receive from the indexes you ultimately select in order to make a profit.

Therefore, because your upside will *always* be contractually limited in some manner, the performance of the indexes you select will not vary that much.

❖ *Why then are companies offering so many different indexes for people like me to choose from?*

After interviewing industry insiders, it became clear that companies do so for marketing and sales purposes to create excitement for both their advisors and the public.

By adding new indexes, companies give annuity advisors something to differentiate their offerings from those of other companies.

New indexes can be exciting, like adding a gold index for example. The purpose is to make annuity purchasers like you enthusiastic about picking a winning index even though your choice won't likely do any better than the others you could have selected.

In the end, because insurance companies are not allowed to take excessive risks, and have had years of experience in what rates of return they have to make to show a profit, any index they offer must be within certain limits; which results in similar rates of return.

❖ *How does the insurance company calculate the percentage my annuity receives based on the index I select?*

The answer to this question is what the rest of this chapter is all about.

❖ *Why does this simple question require an entire chapter for its answer?*

Entire books have been written attempting to answer it. We hope this *Guide* captures the essence of and eliminates most all of the technical jargon and technicalities.

❖ *What's the first thing I need to know about how companies credit interest to my annuity?*

You need to know the period of time—the term—over which the index you select is to be measured. Typically, it is measured monthly, annually, or over a period of two or more years.

❖ *Does the term I select matter?*

Generally, the longer the term—two years or more—the greater the likelihood that you will enjoy better results.

❖ **Will an insurance company credit my annuity with all of an index's increases in value?**

No, they will never do that. They will only credit your annuity with a portion of the increase in the index or indexes you select.

❖ **Why can't the insurance company credit my annuity with all of an index's increase?**

In essence, life insurance companies cannot pay your annuity 100 percent of your index's increase in value, because they would surely lose money, and go bankrupt.

More specifically, because of the mandate required by their guarantees to you, insurance companies are required by law to make the bulk of their investments in conservative investments—long-term, high quality bonds—and can only make a small percentage investment—usually around 5 percent—in their index investments.

Because of these limitations on index investment and their need to make a profit, companies have had to contractually reduce the percentage of what your annuity receives.

❖ **What are the primary ways an insurance company limits the percentage my annuity receives from index increases?**

There are three basic ways life insurance companies limit your annuity's index increases:

1. Some companies set a maximum limit—or **cap rate**—on the percentage of interest your annuity can earn during the term you choose—usually within a given month, year, or over a period that is two years or more as we said earlier.

For example, assume the index you chose is up 10 percent over the term you chose, and your contract has an 8 percent cap. Your annuity would only be credited with 8 percent— the limit under your cap. It will not be allowed to earn any greater percentage than the cap regardless of how well the index performed.

2. They also limit your ability to fully participate in increases in index value by what they call a **participation rate**.

   This means that your right to "participate" in increased index value is limited by a maximum percentage your annuity is allowed to receive.

   For example, if your contract provides for an 80 percent participation rate, and your index goes up 10 percent, you would only be credited with 8 percent (80% x 10%).

3. Companies can also limit your ability to fully participate in index increases with what they call a **spread**.

   With a spread the company subtracts a stated percentage from your index gains during the specified period. A spread does the same thing as a cap, but just applies the formula the opposite way.

   For example, if your contract has a 2 percent spread and the index increases 10 percent, your annuity would only be credited with 8 percent (10% minus the spread of 2% = 8%).

❖ *Aren't these limiting devices just penalties?*

No; they are just limiting tools or "modifiers" to make sure that both the company and you can make money.

It is important for you to understand that *one or more* of these modifiers will always be found in every indexed annuity contract regardless of the company you choose.

❖ *Are you saying that a company can limit my annuity's right to receive index increases with more than one of these modifiers?*

Yes, that is exactly what we are saying.

It is common for companies to combine a cap rate with a participation rate, or to combine a spread with a participation rate. They do not combine a cap rate with a spread, because these two limitations accomplish the same thing—they just do it from opposite ends of the calculation.

❖ *Do some companies offer 100 percent participation rates?*

Yes they do, but when they do, they will be forced to lower your cap rate or increase your spread by the same ratio to make sure they still can make a profit. The bottom line is that your annuity will not receive 100 percent of the increase in an index's appreciation.

❖ *Do companies often set higher cap rates so that I can receive more interest, but then also reduce my participation rate so that what my annuity receives pretty much remains the same?*

They do so all the time.

❖ *Why do companies make how my annuity receives income so complicated?*

We asked this question of industry insiders, and learned that insurance companies have to be concerned about marketing and sales perspectives in order to make annuities appealing to annuity purchasers like you.

Simply put, *"It's good for business to describe the moon and then bring the contract terms back down to earth"* with contractual limitations.

❖ *Are you saying that the returns on indexed annuities aren't any good?*

Not at all! If you keep in mind that you want your money to exceed bank savings returns; and to equal or, perhaps, exceed what you could earn with a fixed annuity by 1 to 2 percentage points, indexed annuities might be appealing to you.

> *For example, if the interest rate on a CD is 2 percent, and the interest rate in your annuity is 4 percent, the percentage increase would be 100 percent.*

❖ *Should I be aware of these limitations in comparing different company contracts?*

Absolutely. There are hundreds of companies, and each has its unique way of combining their cap, participation, and spread limitations.

In fact, it is common for companies to offer a variety of annuity products that differ based on these variables along with many other variables that we will discuss shortly.

❖ *Are we pretty much done talking about the complications in how money grows inside of my annuity?*

We are just getting started, because in addition to limitation modifiers, we also have to discuss the various crediting methods by which increases in index values are actually paid to your annuity.

❖ What are crediting methods?

Crediting methods are the specific choices you make on how you want your annuity to take advantage of the increases in the value of the indexes you select.

❖ How many choices do I have?

In the year 2000, there were 42 separate crediting methods used by life insurance companies. Today, given the popularity of indexed products, there are at least eighty companies offering indexed annuities—each with its own product variations on how they work—making the number of crediting options staggering.

❖ That's overwhelming to me; what's the reality of how I make my choices?

We would suggest that you first reduce your options by only considering highly rated companies, and then further reduce your options by considering only companies that meet your **time horizon**, which is the length of time your annuity must stay in force until you can take your money out without surrender charges.

❖ Will doing so reduce my options to just a handful of crediting options?

It will reduce them substantially, but unfortunately, it won't reduce them to a workable number, because there will still be too many for you to consider.

Here is where your annuity advisor has to buckle down and go with "Vince Lombardi-like essentials"—the running, blocking, and tackling of choosing among the basic crediting options.

❖ *What are the basic crediting options?*

There are three basic ways life insurance companies credit index interest to your annuity. These encompass practically all of the myriad available options:

1. **Point-to-point crediting method**: Your index-linked interest, if any, is based on the *difference* between the index's value at the end of the term you select and the index's value at the start of that term. Interest is added to your annuity at the end of the term.

   Since interest cannot be calculated before the end of the term, use of this design may result in a higher participation rate than annuities using other designs. A higher participation rate means that your annuity will receive more interest.

2. **High-water-mark crediting method**: Your index-linked interest, if any, is determined by looking at the index's value at various points during the term, and is based on the difference between its highest value during the term and the index value when you started.

   Since interest is calculated using the highest value of the index during a term, it may result in higher interest than some other designs if the index reaches a high point early or in the middle of the term, then drops off at the end of the term.

3. **Annual-reset crediting method**: With this method, your index-linked interest, if any, is determined each year by comparing the index value at the end of the contract year with the index value at the start of that contract year, and giving you credit for the difference if it is greater.

Since the interest earned is "locked in" annually and the index value is "reset" at the end of each year, future decreases in the index will not affect the interest you have already earned. Therefore, the annual reset method may result in greater interest crediting than annuities using other methods, when the index fluctuates up and down during the term if it is longer than a year. This design is more likely than others to give you access to index-linked interest before the term ends.

❖ *Wow, it is hard to keep these different choices straight. How important is it that I do so?*

As you will soon find out, we do not believe it is important for you to remember them.

❖ *Why shouldn't I try to memorize them?*

Regardless of what crediting method you select, your interest will be reduced by either your participation rate, cap rate, spread, or a combination of them, to finally give you an indexed interest amount that will be credited to your annuity.

Because of how these limiting modifiers work together, the end result will pretty much be the same regardless of the crediting option you select.

❖ *How can the end result possibly be the same with so many different options?*

Again, life insurance companies are guaranteeing your principal, and are restricted to investing roughly 95 percent of your premium in quality long-term bonds.

Their actuaries—the experts configuring all of these various options—work backwards to make sure that each and every combination of options ends up producing the same calculated results that will make the company the earnings it needs to stay in business, protect your principal, and provide you with a reasonable expectation to receive an upside return.

❖ *Are you specifically saying my selection of crediting method options doesn't much matter in the scheme of things?*

We are saying, in the macro sense, your selection is not going to make a significant difference in what index-linked interest your annuity ends up earning.

However, we are not saying that it doesn't make any difference, because it does. There are always some annuities at any given time in the marketplace that stand out from the others because they produce slightly better returns in tandem with good ratings.

❖ *Do annuity advisors know that the selection of annuity crediting methods doesn't much matter?*

We believe that informed advisors do. Here's a quote by Sheryl Moore—a well-regarded industry teacher—from her article "What's the Best":[4]

> "This same question is asked by nearly everyone when they get started in this business, 'Which indexed crediting method is the best?' Well, that depends. What is your definition of 'best?' The simplest to explain? The easiest to calculate? The most widely-used? The best-performing?

> "If you answered 'yes' to any of these, allow me to drop some knowledge on the subject matter.

"All indexed annuities are priced to return the same amount over a long period of time, regardless of index, crediting method, crediting frequency, or whether the interest is limited via Participation Rates, Caps or Spreads. So, allocate your clients' indexed annuity premiums to an S&P 500® annual point-to-point strategy with a Participation Rate or a Russell 2000 monthly averaging strategy with a Spread. In the long haul, they'll both perform about the same.

"Some say, 'I had a client using XYZ method in 2009, and they earned over 20 percent, but my clients using ABC method were lucky to get zero.' To be clear, some methods will perform better than others from one year to the next. Some will earn zero, while others will earn double-digit gains, but they're all likely to perform somewhere between these two extremes.

"In the long run, the returns will average out to be 1 percent to 2 percent greater interest than average fixed annuity rates on the policy's issue date."

❖ *How can I determine what companies and products, if any, might stand out as best for me?*

That's where you rely on the knowledge and expertise of your annuity advisor.

❖ *I don't know much about annuities, but I do know some companies guarantee a greater interest rate than others. Given what you have said, shouldn't I try to find the best interest rate and be done with it?*

While we understand your point, we feel strongly that you should first look at the company that is issuing the annuity. Each life insurance company is rated by several agencies. We believe you should only consider companies that have an "A" in their ratings.

Lesser-rated companies often offer better performing products by reducing the limitations on their index performance. By selecting one of them, you will almost always be trading more potential gain for less potential safety. We believe in the **safety-first rule**: Preservation of principal is more important than increasing returns by increasing risk.

If you are *not* particularly concerned about the preservation of your principal, we believe that you would be better served in the securities markets where there are no guarantees, but far superior upsides when markets are up; and that you consider a variable annuity.

❖ *Given the incredible number of choices available, how can my advisor possibly know what company, products, and crediting methods will stand out and be best for me?*

He or she has access to sophisticated software that makes all the comparisons and calculations necessary to provide you with the best available options at that time.

❖ *Does it matter what computer programs my advisor relies upon?*

In our view it matters a lot:

- Insurance companies have software that is free to advisors.

- The middlemen between the companies and the advisors—they are called insurance marketing organizations—also offer their advisors free software.

- Additionally, advisors can pay to subscribe to one or more independent services offering specialized annuity comparison software programs.

We believe that if your advisor uses an independent computerized service, there will be far more choices, and far less bias, in determining the options that are best for you.

Chapter Highlights

1. Make sure that the company you select is trustworthy in terms of its guarantee. In our view this means that your advisor should recommend companies with an "A" in their rating.

2. Understand the limiting modifications companies impose on your earnings, regardless of what indexes you select or by what method earnings will be credited to your annuity. They are easily identified as the participation, cap, and spread rates.

3. Regardless of all of the choices available to you, the results attained by each of them will be just about the same over time.

4. An indexed annuity will likely earn 1 to 2 percent more than a fixed annuity, and most likely perform better than CDs based on documented history.

CHAPTER 6

Income Riders

An income rider is an added feature attached to a fixed or indexed annuity that provides an extra source of income for you. The rider's interest rate is significantly in excess of the annuity contract's guaranteed rate and also far greater than the annual declared rates that companies have paid since the Great Recession.

In researching income riders, we have come to believe that they are the most talked about, lauded, attacked, misunderstood, and popular indexed annuity option other than, perhaps, annuity **bonuses**.

❖ *Why do you say they are misunderstood?*

The literature that talks about them is difficult to understand:

- Company literature, whether in promotional brochures or the language within the riders themselves, is filled with jargon that is not fully understandable for non-experts.

- The writings of industry experts—mostly actuaries trained in mathematics—are incredibly complex, and definitely not understandable other than to fellow actuaries.

- The hundreds of articles and blogs written by advisors extolling their virtues are chock full of superlatives, but generally do not explain how those "superlatives" actually work—even though they may work well.

- Most of the articles and blogs criticizing them do not provide the logical detail to meaningfully make their case.

In this chapter we are going to do our best to give you an understanding of the basic mechanics of how income riders work and how they can best perform for you.

❖ Why are income riders popular today?

They are incredibly popular, because with the guarantees on fixed and indexed products hovering around 2 percent, and income riders ranging between 6 and 8 percent, annuity advisors can make the obvious case for touting their virtues.

❖ What considerations should I discuss with my advisor if I am thinking about purchasing an income rider?

At a minimum, you should discuss these basic questions:

- To what extent are you concerned about the loss of your principal?

- Do you need an income stream now, or later when you retire?

- How much income do you anticipate needing?

- When do you anticipate needing your annuity funds?

- Do you want to leave your retirement money to your family?

- How much can you afford to spend?

❖ *What are income riders designed to accomplish?*

First, and foremost, they are designed to generate an enhanced income stream when you retire. Secondly, they are designed, at least to some degree, to create a near-term income stream.

❖ *What do you mean by a near-term income stream?*

Traditionally, a near term income stream was addressed by a **single-premium immediate annuity (SPIA)**—not like a deferred indexed or fixed annuity. With interest rates at historical lows, SPIAs are not as attractive as they were when interest rates were 5 percent or higher; thereby making an income rider an alternative that may be worthwhile for you to consider.

❖ *What is an income rider's primary attribute?*

Advisors and clients are looking to the higher interest rates offered by income riders relative to the lower interest rates that have been with us since 2008. The company may also offer a bonus on the income base if you purchase one.

❖ *Can you tell me more about bonuses that are paid on income riders?*

We discuss them fully in chapter 8, but here is a short synopsis:

- Bonuses are currently offered by many companies.

- You do not receive the bonus as a cash payment.

- They range from 4 to 12 percent on the money you put into your base contract.

- They limit your upside potential to make sure the company still makes its profit.

- They are credited to your base contract from day one, and not to your rider's income base.

❖ What advantage do income riders have over SPIAs?

Income riders allow you to keep control over your principal to a greater extent than SPIAs. When you purchase a SPIA, you **annuitize** your money immediately. When you annuitize your money, you lock in your payments of principal and income, and no longer have control over what you can do with your principal.

Income riders also lock in higher interest rates compared to the interest rate annuitized in your SPIA; but do not annuitize your contract.

❖ Do income riders pay out more or less than SPIAs?

Generally a little less; but this is not the real question.

❖ What's the real question?

There are really two important questions:

1. Do you need income now or later?

2. If you do need income later, what is your ability to exercise control over your principal?

❖ How do income riders give me control?

Most income riders allow you to start, stop, restart, and again stop when taking lifetime income withdrawals from your income base. You do not have set distributions; you decide if and when to take withdrawals.

❖ *Is an income rider useful if I'm looking for the best way to guarantee an income stream on my retirement, which is years away?*

This is its most ideal use.

❖ *Are income riders available for both fixed and indexed annuities?*

Yes, but they are most often found with indexed annuities.

❖ *Do income riders change the terms and conditions of my base indexed contract?*

No, they do not; they are simply an addition to it.

❖ *What if interest rates spike up after I buy an income rider? Does my interest rate go up in the rider itself, or in my base contract, or in both?*

Your interest rate will never go lower than the rate you purchased in your income rider, but it could increase if your earnings in the base annuity outperform the interest rate in the income rider. With most carriers, you will receive the higher of the two rates for that year.

❖ *Can I cancel or remove an income rider at any time?*

Some income riders are cancellable while others are not. Your advisor will be able to answer this question based on the riders that interest you.

❖ What do income riders cost?

Usually somewhere between ¾ to 1 percent—annuity advisors talk about their cost in terms of 75 to 100 basis points (1 basis point equals 1/100th of a percent).

❖ How does my annuity get charged for the cost of the rider?

The percentage is multiplied against your base contract, but the insurance company takes your rider fee from your stated earnings. Some riders only charge a fee if you have earnings in the base annuity, while most charge a fee regardless of whether there are earnings in the base contract.

❖ Is this a one-time fee or does the insurance company continue to take an annual fee for every year of the rider's term?

The fee continues for the term of your rider.

❖ When are the fees paid?

They are generally collected on a monthly basis, starting thirty days after the date you buy the rider, and continue all the way through the term of your payment schedule, or until the rider is cancelled.

❖ Do the fees end at my death?

They do, unless you select a joint-and-survivor income option for you and your spouse; in which case they stop at the death of your surviving spouse.

❖ **Is it possible for my income rider fee to actually generate a loss in my base contract for the year?**

Hypothetically, yes, if the fee is greater than your actual earnings. However, some companies only assess a fee if there is gain in the base contract to cover it.

❖ **Does my advisor receive a commission for selling an income rider?**

No, we have not found an income rider where a company pays an additional commission to an advisor.

❖ **How soon can I start receiving income from my rider?**

With most companies, you can start one year after its purchase; but with some companies you can do so immediately.

It is important for you to remember that most income riders are designed to compound over longer periods of time—creating a long-term additional income benefit—rather than an immediate one.

❖ **If I purchase an income rider, do I have to elect to take payments for life or can I convert to a SPIA and annuitize my base contract?**

If after you purchase an income rider you want to convert to a SPIA, you will be able to do so with your accumulated value—less surrender charges if any—in your base annuity. However, you will forfeit the build-up in your income account created by the rider.

❖ *Are you saying that I lose the income build-up I paid for if I want to annuitize my indexed annuity?*

Yes, that is what we are saying.

❖ *If I purchase an income rider, does my accumulation account still go up by the greater of its guaranteed rate or the actual earnings paid to it by the company?*

Yes, it does.

❖ *Do I purchase an income rider for a specific number of years?*

Yes you do, and that is called its "term." The term is generally ten years or longer.

❖ *Can I purchase my income rider for a term greater than ten years?*

Yes; you can purchase it for a ten-year term and then your contract can provide a right for you to renew it for another ten years, for a total of twenty years. However, with many companies this right ceases when you attain the age of 80 or 85 years.

❖ *When my income term is over, will my income account stop compounding?*

Yes; your income will stop compounding at the **roll-up rate**, but you will continue to receive any earnings at your base contract rate.

❖ **Can I purchase an income rider if I am not forty years of age?**

No, forty is typically the threshold age requirement.

❖ **Why do companies have a threshold age limit?**

They do not want your income account to compound for too many years, because they would not be able to ensure the rate of return for such a protracted period of time.

❖ **Are there surrender charges if I take income for life too soon?**

Unlike your basic contract, there are *no surrender charges in your income rider.* This is a major feature of income riders that allows you to control your principal.

❖ **Is my income rider account calculated with simple or compound interest?**

Most, but not all, companies compound interest in their income account calculations. You have to be careful if you select a company's rider that is paying a significantly higher rate than most other companies.

❖ **Why do I have to be careful?**

The higher rate may be a simple rate rather than a compound one, which makes a huge difference as to what your annuity ultimately makes.

❖ *If I purchase a guaranteed income rider, can I still elect to convert my income account to a SPIA later?*

No; you can only convert your accumulated value in your base contract to a SPIA, and cannot do so with your income account.

❖ *What happens to my income rider on conversion to a SPIA?*

The income rider is terminated and there is no value.

❖ *Can you refresh my memory as to the difference between a SPIA and an income rider?*

A SPIA is an annuity that begins paying an annuitized income stream immediately. The payments consist of principal and interest for a stated number of years, or over your lifetime, or over the lifetimes of you and your spouse in the amounts determined by actuarial tables. The income rate is fixed.

Guaranteed income for life generated from an income rider is not annuitized under the actuarial tables, and will be paid back to you based upon the table in your rider that specifies what percent of the income base you can take at the age you elect to take it.

Unlike your payments that are annuitized, all of the distributions you receive from your income rider will be subject to ordinary income tax until there is no income left in your account.

❖ *So, are you saying that if I elect to start taking income for life under my income rider, I won't be getting the exclusion ratio with all of my payments?*

We are; you will lose the exclusion ratio.

❖ **Do companies offer a cost of living adjustment for my rider?**

Some do, and their payout rates are initially lower when income for life is taken—compared to not having the cost of living adjustment; but those payments can increase over time under the terms of the cost of living adjustment.

❖ **Does my income rider stop at my death?**

As we discussed earlier, it generally does; but some companies offer an additional death benefit that accumulates at higher interest rates for your beneficiaries.

❖ **If my income rider stops at my death, can my base annuity continue under the options I selected?**

Yes, it can. The terms of your base contract are separate from your income rider.

❖ **Do income riders have additional benefits for my long-term care?**

Generally, they do not. However, some companies will increase income payments if extended long-term-care situations occur, and can be documented.

❖ **Can I elect a joint income payout for both my life and my spouse's life?**

Yes, and you don't have to make the decision until you decide to turn the income on under your rider.

❖ *In terms of a company's accounting, what happens after I purchase an income rider?*

The company sets up an imaginary accounting account, which is generally known as your **income account**; but each company has its own name for this account.

❖ *Wait a minute, do you really mean it when you describe my income account as "imaginary"?*

The account is imaginary in that no funds are in the account. The company simply makes an accounting entry that reflects the interest rate that your income rider provides. This interest rate is called the **roll-up rate** and is used for the time period in your rider.

Your roll-up-rate interest is credited to the account annually; but the actual cash is not available until you begin taking your lifetime income payments, and then only after you have exhausted your principal in your base account, along with its guaranteed and actual earnings.

❖ *Why don't people like me know about these accounting mechanics?*

This enigma is what we alluded to at the very beginning of this chapter.

The income account is "on the books" of the company as an accounting entry. The company guarantees that it will make good on the amount shown in the account. For more information about the guarantee, see Chapter 3, How Good Are Life Insurance Company Guarantees?

❖ *So are you saying that if I buy an 8 percent income rider, I am not actually earning 8 percent on my annuity's principal?*

Your income account is compounding at 8 percent on an accounting basis, but you can only take income payments under the terms of the withdrawal schedule in your income rider contract.

❖ *Does the company limit my income payments?*

Yes, it does so according to a withdrawal table in your rider that limits how much of your income base you can take out annually.

❖ *What is this withdrawal table based on?*

It is based on your attained age when you start taking withdrawals—the older you are, the greater the percentage that you will be able to withdraw, because of the fewer number of years you are projected to live under life expectancy tables.

❖ *How quickly can I take my income account out under the withdrawal tables of most companies?*

Generally, the average is around 5 percent per year, but that number may increase according to your age at the time you turn on the income spigot.

❖ *Can I take my income account out in a lump sum?*

No.

❖ *So, even though I purchased an income rider, and the company sets up an income account for me for accounting purposes, the distributions I receive will first be made from the principal and guaranteed income in my base contract's accumulated account?*

Yes, you have it. For every dollar you take under your payment schedule, you are reducing your accumulated value in your base contract by that dollar amount.

❖ *Is there a death benefit if I don't take all of the money out of my income-for-life account?*

With very few exceptions, there is no death benefit from the income account; only the remaining accumulation value, if any, within the base annuity may be paid to your beneficiaries.

❖ *Will my income rider keep paying me for as long as I live, even if I significantly outlive my life expectancy?*

It will! This is a truly wonderful feature of income riders. Hopefully it was the essence of what you bargained for when you added it to your base annuity.

❖ *When do income riders really work well?*

They work extremely well if you live a long time, because you will receive many years of income payments over and above the return of your principal and its built-in base earnings.

Chapter Highlights

1. An income rider is a feature of an indexed annuity that provides additional income that is significantly in excess of an annuity's guaranteed rate.

2. Income riders allow you to keep control over your principal to a greater extent than SPIAs.

3. Your interest rate will never go lower than the rate you purchased in your income rider, but it could increase if your earnings in the base annuity outperform the interest rate in the income rider.

4. The insurance company does not actually fund the income rider amount; it tracks the account and the interest it makes using an accounting entry on its books.

5. There are limits on how much you can receive under your income rider that are set out in your contract.

6. Income riders, while very effective planning tools, are complex and offer a number of options; so it is important that you work with your advisor to determine if an income rider is right for you.

CHAPTER 7

Long-Term-Care Riders

Long-term care (LTC) has become a major issue with the aging of America's baby boomers. According to the U.S. Census Bureau, by 2030 there will be 71 million people age 64 or older; twice as many as there were in 2000. Nearly one in five Americans will be eighty years or older.

Statistics vary, but the Family Caregiver Alliance® offers the following:

- The lifetime probability of becoming disabled in at least two activities of daily living (ADLs) or of being cognitively impaired is 68 percent for people age 65 and older.

- By 2050, the number of individuals using paid LTC services in any setting (e.g., at home or in assisted living or skilled nursing facilities) will likely double from the thirteen million using services in 2000, to 27 million people.

- Of the older population with LTC needs in the community, about 30 percent (1.5 million persons) have substantial LTC needs (three or more ADL limitations). Of these, about 25 percent are 85 and older, and 70 percent report they are in fair to poor health.

❖ *Shouldn't I consider an LTC insurance policy?*

Most people are familiar with their opportunity to purchase an LTC policy, and you should look into purchasing one. It is not our purpose to cover LTC insurance. Our purpose is to give you a sense of what opportunities exist for LTC coverage within your annuity.

We encourage you to seek the services of your annuity advisor to recommend an LTC specialist to determine whether coverage in your case *would be better purchased within your annuity* or outside of it through a stand-alone LTC policy.

❖ *I have never heard about annuities that have LTC coverage. What are they?*

You are not alone. Many people are not aware of their opportunity to purchase a **long-term-care rider** that attaches to a fixed or indexed annuity or to purchase a **hybrid annuity** that includes LTC coverage.

In this chapter, we treat LTC riders and hybrid annuities as one and the same; and refer to them as "LTC riders," unless there are specific features that need differentiation, in which case we will call them by their proper names.

❖ *Is it true that if I have difficulty purchasing an LTC policy, I might be able to get coverage issued more easily through an annuity rider?*

Yes, that is true. The health underwriting standards for riders are less stringent and relatively fast. In addition, the underwriting process for an LTC rider is simpler than the underwriting for a traditional LTC policy.

❖ *Can I purchase an LTC rider without having to go through any medical questions or tests?*

No, that is not very likely. Most companies require you to answer a simple set of questions, usually around twelve or less, that are about the state of your over-all health. The company will not go into great detail, or require a medical examination.

❖ *Should I consider purchasing a fixed or indexed annuity specifically to take advantage of its LTC rider?*

No, that should not be your single purpose. If your LTC consideration is important enough as an added reason or "tipping point" in your decision to purchase an annuity, you should definitely consider doing so.

If you are not healthy enough to qualify for an LTC insurance policy because your condition may shorten your life span, then you should consider this question: "Why would you purchase an annuity if your health is so bad as to cause your premature death?" Since an annuity is for the long-term, it would be a major error to purchase one if you have a shortened life expectancy.

❖ *If I receive any LTC benefits from my rider, will they be income taxable to me?*

No, they will be income-tax free.

❖ *If I transfer an old annuity into my existing one with an LTC rider, are there any adverse income tax consequences?*

No, there are none.

❖ *Is there an age limit on my ability to purchase an LTC rider?*

Companies differ on their maximum age, but generally center around age eighty.

❖ *What do LTC riders generally cost?*

The charges vary by company and how they assess the charge. Some companies assess the charge against your annuity's accumulation amount; others subtract it from the declared interest rate each year—for example, 1 percent per year is subtracted from the company's declared rate. The charge is usually taken monthly.

❖ *Can the insurance company increase the cost of my LTC rider after I purchase it?*

They cannot; unlike traditional LTC policy premiums which the insurance company can increase. This feature is major, as our review of the literature suggests that many companies have been forced to significantly increase their LTC insurance premiums because of the unexpected proliferation and size of claims.

❖ *If I am receiving LTC benefits under my annuity's LTC coverage, will I still be charged a fee?*

Your LTC charges will be waived during the period in which you are receiving benefits.

❖ *Will the cost of my LTC rider generally be less than a stand-alone LTC policy?*

The literature says it should be "considerably" less than a stand-alone policy that provides similar payouts. Our research leads us to believe that it depends on the situation, and that you should discuss the costs and benefits of both alternatives with your annuity advisor and an LTC specialist.

❖ Do I receive LTC benefits immediately if I need them, or do I have to satisfy a waiting period?

Again, it depends upon the company, but generally you will not be able to claim benefits prior to your rider being in effect for at least one to two years.

❖ For how long can I receive benefit payments?

That also varies by company, but in most cases you will receive monthly payments for up to six years.

❖ How are my monthly benefits determined?

The conventional formula is:

LTC maximum coverage is divided by the number of coverage months to determine your monthly maximum.

❖ What events will trigger my LTC rider's payments?

Generally, your payments will be triggered when you cannot perform two or three of the six ADLs; or are cognitively impaired, as determined by one or more licensed medical professionals.

❖ What services are generally covered by my LTC rider?

Usually, the same services that are covered in traditional policies are covered by LTC riders, including residence in an assisted living facility or nursing home, adult day care, and home-health-care services.

❖ *How is the amount of my coverage determined?*

Generally, you will be eligible to receive a multiple of the accumulation value in your annuity's account that ranges from an increase of 150 to 300 percent of its value. The sales literature refers to these increases as **leveraging factors.**

❖ *Are there maximum limits on the benefits I can receive?*

There are, for the maximum amount of your monthly payments and for the maximum number of months that you can receive payments. All of this information is contained in your rider agreement.

❖ *Where do my LTC payments come from?*

For the most part, they first reduce your accumulated account value until it is exhausted, and then continue from the insurance company until your coverage limit has been reached.

❖ *If the company is reducing my account balance first, aren't I paying the company a fee to pay me back my own money?*

You are, at least until those monies are exhausted. After that, you are receiving the company's money up to the rider maximum, which will likely be two to three times the amount in your accumulation account. If it's helpful for you, remember, you are insuring long-term needs rather than short-term ones.

❖ *Is there a surrender charge schedule that applies to my LTC rider?*

Yes, in hybrid annuities it is generally covered by your annuity's base surrender charge schedule. In cases where the rider is purchased separately, it may have its own surrender charge schedule or refer to the schedule in the annuity it attaches to.

❖ *Am I charged surrender penalties for my LTC benefit payments?*

No, surrender charges do not apply to your payments.

❖ *If I want additional protection against inflation, can I purchase an inflation rider on my LTC rider?*

Yes; it will be for an additional cost, and will have to be purchased when you purchase the rider.

❖ *Can I elect to pay for joint LTC coverage for myself and my spouse?*

Generally you can. The coverage will be there for your joint LTC needs for a maximum combined period—say one hundred months; but if you are both receiving LTC payments at the same time, the payment period will be cut in half, since you are doubling up on the benefits you will be receiving.

❖ *Can I purchase an LTC rider that will make payments for my life?*

Our research has uncovered limited claims for such, but we have not seen a payout-for-life policy. Your annuity advisor will assist you in locating such a policy.

❖ Can there be a death benefit with an LTC rider?

Yes, there can. Generally your beneficiaries will receive a death benefit that is the greater of your annuity's accumulated value, less the LTC benefits the company paid out to you.

❖ Is an LTC rider a better choice than a stand-alone LTC policy?

This question cannot be answered without making the specific comparisons and doing the math. So, we end where we started: Your annuity advisor will likely recommend an LTC specialist to do a comparison of the costs and benefits.

Chapter Highlights

1. You can purchase a long-term-care rider that attaches to a fixed or indexed annuity or to purchase a hybrid annuity that includes LTC coverage.

2. The health underwriting standards for LTC riders are less stringent, relatively faster, and simpler than the underwriting standards for a traditional LTC policy.

3. Obtaining LTC coverage should not be your single reason for purchasing an annuity, but it can be an important factor in your decision-making process.

4. LTC rider distributions are first applied to your accumulated account value until it is exhausted, and thereafter from your insurance company.

5. LTC riders come with a cost, and should always be compared to a traditional LTC insurance policy by an LTC expert.

· CHAPTER 8 ·

Bonuses

Annuity **bonuses** are payments from the insurance company that add money to your fixed or indexed annuity's base contract amount at the time of your purchase.

Just like the advertisements on television, "But wait, there's more, much more…," companies use the enticement of adding their bonus payments to your new annuity as a marketing stratagem; and also as a very effective—and worthy—sales incentive.

In the case of bonuses, "there is more," because they have real merit. However, as with all things "annuity," bonuses have some complications that we will tell you about that can affect other moving parts in your annuity contract.

It is our hope that by reading this chapter, you will gain an essential grasp of the benefits that bonuses can provide to you along with an appreciation of their limitations.

❖ *Why do insurance companies offer bonuses?*

In the highly competitive annuity market, companies are forced to offer incentives to differentiate their products, and make them more attractive. Bonuses are a feature designed to do just that.

❖ *How much is a typical bonus?*

The bonus is based on a percentage of the premium you pay when purchasing your annuity. As we write this, companies are paying bonuses between 1 and 12 percent.

❖ *How can insurance companies afford to pay such high bonuses?*

Companies offer bonuses with the hope that purchasers like you will keep their funds in their annuities long enough for the companies to receive profitable returns.

Over time, your insurance company will earn back the value of the bonus it paid you. One disparaging article that referred to bonuses was titled "Annuity 'Bonus' is Like Tooth Fairy's Tale," because insurance companies have to make a profit on their bonus money; so in reality, it is nothing more than their loan—at a profit—to you. You do not get something for nothing.

❖ *What accounts for such a broad range of payments?*

First, and foremost, the aggressiveness of the company. More aggressive companies—those that pay higher bonuses—are rated lower by the rating agencies than more conservative ones.

Second, the higher-paying companies usually limit their participation and cap rates for indexed annuities so that they can pay the bonuses and remain profitable.

❖ *Do they pay me the money or add it to my annuity's principal?*

They add it to your annuity's accumulation account.

❖ *Do most insurance companies offer bonuses?*

Yes, and increasingly so. They offer them because the bonus feature has proven to be the "hottest" marketing feature in the fixed and indexed annuity marketplace.

❖ *Why are they so popular?*

They are a compelling marketing incentive because insurance companies add their money to yours at the very beginning of the contract period, and compound your annuity's earnings on the bonus money and your contributed money.

❖ *Do bonuses always get paid when the initial contribution is made to an annuity?*

They are always credited to your account contemporaneously with your premium deposit. Some companies even credit your annuity with the bonus percentage when you make additional contributions to your annuity.

❖ *What is the most common reason for people to buy annuities that offer a bonus?*

Most people buy annuities with bonuses to offset the possible cost of surrender charges when they want to exchange or roll over an older annuity into a new one with better terms. In doing so, they compare the amount of the bonus against the surrender charge, if any, in the older annuity.

They also use the bonus payment as a justification for purchasing a fixed or indexed annuity, if they are experiencing underperforming investments in other sectors.

❖ Are there age limits on who can receive bonuses?

Most bonuses are available until ages ranging between 75 and 85.

❖ Are these bonuses only offered on a one-time basis?

Most fixed and indexed annuities are offered only on premiums paid in the first year of the annuity contract.

❖ Are there multi-year bonuses that add money to my annuity for a number of years after I purchase it?

Yes; some companies offer **multi-year bonuses** for additional deposits made, up to seven years.

❖ Are the multi-year payments less than the one-time, up-front bonus?

Some insurance companies offer premium bonuses as high as 10 percent on *all deposits* made within five to seven years.

❖ Are the bonuses my annuity receives included in calculations of my annuity's death benefit, minimum guaranteed surrender value, and ultimate cash surrender value?

Yes, in most all cases.

❖ Do some annuity bonuses vest over a period of years?

They do.

❖ *Do bonus payments fluctuate with market conditions?*

They do.

❖ *If I am due to receive bonus payments in years subsequent to my purchase, and bonus rates go up, can I get paid the higher bonus rate in those years?*

No.

❖ *Does my bonus have a separate surrender charge schedule different from my base annuity's surrender charge schedule?*

Yes, and they are becoming more and more frequent. They are called **recapture charges**.

❖ *Does my annuity's surrender charge schedule also apply to the bonus?*

Yes, it does; and in some cases, will take away the entire bonus when combined with the bonus schedule.

❖ *What do bonuses really cost?*

As we stated earlier, they don't cost you anything at the time they are credited to your account.

They do have a cost over a period of years, however, and you can lose money on them if you terminate your contract during the surrender charge period.

❖ *What do they cost over the years?*

They come at a cost of a lower declared rate if you have a fixed annuity, and a lower participation and cap rate if you have an indexed annuity.

❖ *What are the effects of lowering my participation rate or cap rate?*

Your annuity will not perform as well as it would have without the bonus payment.

❖ *Can my annuity receive a bonus if I select a systematic withdrawal plan when I set it up?*

Yes.

❖ *Comparing apples to apples, am I better off with or without a bonus payment in my annuity?*

Tell us how long you are going to live. If you live a longer time, you are likely to make less because of the many years of lower participation and cap rates. Conversely, if you do not expect to live for your life expectancy because of health reasons, a bonus becomes more attractive.

❖ *This doesn't make sense to me, is there another way to say it?*

Here's another way of saying it that may be more understandable to you: Because, the cost of the bonus is paid for by lower returns to you in the annuity versus not having a bonus, if you die sooner than expected, the bonus may be more beneficial to you.

❖ *What happens to my bonus if I terminate my contract during the surrender period?*

It will be reduced by the applicable surrender charge. That charge is a stated percentage in your contract that is multiplied against your accumulated value, which includes the bonus payment.

❖ *Given the popularity of these bonuses, and the amounts companies are offering to give me, would I be better off terminating an older annuity?*

This is a question that you should ask your annuity advisor after the math is fully worked out to compare the options in your particular case.

❖ *Does an insurance company charge their fees on the additional bonus money placed in my account?*

It does. Its fees are charged on a percentage of your base account and the bonus additions to it.

❖ *Can I also receive a bonus on what I pay for an income rider?*

Yes, some companies will credit your income base with the same percentage that was credited to your accumulation account. Doing this appears to be an up-and-coming trend.

❖ *What happens to my income-rider bonus if I terminate my income rider*

You lose it.

❖ *Since I pay for an income rider each year, do insurance companies give me a bonus on my income account each year?*

No, they do not. The bonus is a one-time payment on an income rider.

❖ *What are the advantages associated with bonuses?*

The can add meaningfully to your annuity's accumulated value.

❖ *Are there caveats I should be worried about?*

There are:

- Lower-rated companies tend to offer higher bonus payments—a trade-off that we recommend you carefully consider.

- Be sure you can live with a greater number of years in the surrender charge schedule.

- Check, compare, and analyze how much lower your participation and cap rates will be compared to your annuity choice without a bonus.

- The bonus payment can be less than the surrender charge you have to pay on terminating an existing annuity.

- The length of your surrender charge period will most always be greater than what it would have been without the bonus.

- Your contract's participation rate and cap rate will most always be lower than they would have been if you didn't receive the bonus.

- If your bonus is paid on your income rider, you will lose it if you terminate the income rider.

Chapter Highlights

1. A bonus is a payment from an insurance company that adds money to your fixed or indexed annuity's base contract amount at the time of your purchase.

2. A bonus is a fixed percentage of your annuity premium and can be a one-time payment or multi-year payments.

3. Bonuses come with costs: Participation and cap rates are lower than with non-bonus annuities, and there may be additional surrender charges.

4. A common use for a bonus is when one annuity is exchanged for another. The bonus is used to fully or partially offset the surrender charge of the annuity that is being replaced.

5. It is extremely important for you and your annuity advisor to do the math to make sure that the bonus will prove to be profitable for you over time.

6. Always check the rating of the insurance company that is offering a bonus; the higher the bonus is, the more likely it is being sold by a lower-rated company.

· CHAPTER 9 ·

The Taxation of Annuities

The income, estate, and gift taxation of annuities has been written about in numerous technical treatises, books, articles, and blogs. As with most tax laws, annuity taxation can be complicated; and in some cases, very complicated.

Our goal is to answer your questions with understandable answers that will give you a sound grasp of the federal tax basics as they apply to fixed and indexed annuities.

❖ *Can I deduct the purchase cost of my annuity?*

No, you cannot; you buy it with after-tax dollars.

❖ *Can my IRA deduct the purchase cost of my annuity?*

No, it cannot.

❖ *Do I or my IRA pay tax on the growth of my annuity while it's accumulating value?*

No; one of your annuity's most significant benefits is the ability to grow its earnings free of income tax during the accumulation period.

❖ *What are the income tax consequences if I purchase an annuity in my traditional IRA, 401(k), or company-sponsored qualified retirement plan?*

Your contributions will go into the plan free of tax, and the earnings will be free of tax while in the plan. When you begin making withdrawals, you will pay regular federal income tax on every dollar you receive, no matter if it is annuity earnings or principal.

❖ *Why do I have to pay tax on every dollar I receive?*

You pay tax on your plan's entire amount as you receive payments, because you never paid tax on either the annuity principal or earnings.

❖ *Is the income taxation of an annuity that I own individually different than one held in my retirement plan?*

Yes, and the method of taxation varies with when and how you take money from your annuity.

❖ *What happens when I annuitize my annuity and start receiving payments for the rest of my life?*

You only pay income tax on a portion of your distributions if you owned your annuity outside of your IRA.

If your IRA owned the annuity, you pay income tax on *all* of your distributions.

❖ *If I own my own annuity, how do I know what percentage of my distributions are attributed to the portion that is taxed?*

The Internal Revenue Code provides you with the benefits of an **exclusion ratio**, which is a formula that allocates a portion of every dollar you receive between tax-free principal and taxable income.

❖ *How does the exclusion ratio work?*

The exclusion ratio calculation is quite complicated and neither you nor most professionals need to understand all of its rules. We will give a simple explanation of the principles of the exclusion ratio, so that you can approximate what percentage of your distributions will be taxable.

The exclusion ratio is based on three factors:

1. Your principal—the amount of contributions

2. Earnings (technically called expected return), which is the difference between the principal and the total value of your annuity when you decide to annuitize it

3. Your life expectancy at the time you begin taking payments

Armed with this information, you can make a quick approximation of your exclusion ratio by dividing the principal you put into the annuity by the total anticipated value of your annuity.

For example, if you paid $100,000 into your annuity, and your statement shows the value of your annuity is $200,000, your exclusion ratio is 50 percent. On this simplified basis, half of each payment is taxable; the other half isn't, because it is the tax-free return of your principal.

You can also ask your insurance company to do a more precise calculation for you.

All annuitized payments that you receive during your life expectancy would be based on this exclusion ratio.

❖ Why doesn't my IRA get the exclusion ratio?

Your IRA bought an annuity on your life with before-tax dollars, and income earned on those dollars is totally taxed deferred. Because of those tax benefits, 100 percent of your IRA distributions will be taxable to you as ordinary income.

❖ How are my annuity payments taxed if I live longer than my life expectancy?

For annuity payments begun after 1987, all payments made after you exceed your life expectancy are ordinary income. In this situation, you have already received all of your principal back, so there is no longer any principal amount to return. For annuity payment begun prior to 1987, the exclusion ratio applies to all payments.

❖ How do I determine the exact amount that I have to pay tax on?

The insurance company will calculate it for you each year in time for tax season, and provide you with a form 1099.

❖ What happens when I receive payments from my annuity during the accumulation period?

All your payments will be taxed as ordinary income until there is only principal remaining in your account. All payments after that will be tax free, because they are distributions of your principal.

This method of taxation is called **LIFO** (last in first out) taxation. The last money in—earnings—is the first to come out.

❖ What if I have an income rider?

Income rider payments are taxed just like distributions during your accumulation period. First the earnings come out, and are taxed. When all of the income is exhausted, the remainder is not subject to tax.

❖ What happens if I transfer an older annuity into a newly purchased one?

You do not pay any tax on the transfer. Done properly, this is called a section **1035 exchange**, which is the section of the Internal Revenue Code that applies to this transaction.

❖ Do annuities have the same early-withdrawal penalty rules as retirement plans?

Yes. You may have to pay a federal penalty tax on any income you withdraw from your annuity if you are under the age of 59½ at the time of your withdrawals.

❖ Is the penalty tax on the total amount of my withdrawals while I'm under the age of 59½?

No, the penalty tax applies only to the income portion.

❖ **What happens if I take distributions when I am older than 59½?**

The penalty does not apply to any distribution you receive after that age.

❖ **If I am disabled, is there a penalty tax if I take money out during the period of my disability?**

No, there is no penalty tax; this is a relatively new and good exception to the general rule.

❖ **What if someone else is the owner of the annuity on my life?**

Whoever is owner will be liable for paying both the regular income tax and the penalty tax.

❖ **What if I elect to take systematic withdrawals?**

As we discussed in chapter 4, you will avoid the penalty tax, because the law has a specific exception for this payment plan. The income tax rules will apply, however.

❖ **Will the insurance company withhold taxes before making payments to me?**

They will, unless you or your advisor tells them not to. The insurance company will require you to fill out a W-9 form.

❖ **What happens if the payments I would have received go instead to one or more of my beneficiaries?**

They will pay tax, just like you would have paid the tax on them.

❖ **Is there a way for me to get capital gains treatment when taking money out of my annuity?**

No; you cannot receive capital gains treatment, regardless of how you receive distributions.

❖ **If I give my annuity to someone else during my lifetime, are there income tax consequences?**

There are.

❖ **How do I calculate my income tax after making a gift of my annuity?**

You must report the entire amount of the gain as ordinary income on your income tax return for the year you made the gift.

❖ **If I transfer my annuity into my revocable living trust, will I have to pay income tax?**

No, this transfer is not a taxable event; but there is rarely a reason to make such a transfer.

❖ **What if I transfer my annuity to my irrevocable trust?**

The transfer will be treated as if you gave it to someone else, and you will have to report the entire amount of the earnings on your tax return as ordinary income.

❖ **Do I owe income taxes if I surrender my annuity?**

Yes, you do. If you fully surrender your annuity, your taxable gain is the amount you receive less your principal amount.

If you make a partial withdrawal, the amount of your taxable gain is the excess of your contract value over your principal amount, which is considered your cost basis, without regard to any surrender charges you have to pay.

❖ **If I have to pay a surrender charge when taking money out of my annuity, can I deduct the charge on my tax return?**

No, you cannot deduct the cost of surrender charges.

❖ **If I or my IRA were to surrender my annuity and it has gone down in value, can I or my IRA deduct the loss as an itemized deduction?**

Fixed and indexed annuities don't have losses due to market changes. The only losses to principal come as a result of a surrender charge exceeding any gains or interest earned in the contract. Upon surrender, the difference between the premium paid and the new surrender value is a qualified personal loss.

❖ *If I own a fixed or indexed annuity outside of my IRA, what are the income tax consequences if I die before taking distributions from it?*

The difference between your original principal value and the total value of the annuity will be taxed as ordinary income to your beneficiaries.

❖ *If my IRA owns my fixed or indexed annuity, what are the income tax consequences if I die before taking distributions from it?*

The entire value of your annuity will be taxed as it is distributed to your beneficiaries.

❖ *If I own my fixed or indexed annuity outside of my IRA, what are the income tax consequences if I die after I started taking distributions from it?*

If your beneficiary receives either a lump sum payout or payments under the payout option you elected, the proceeds will be excluded from their income until the combined amount received by you and them exceeds your principal.

❖ *If my IRA owns my annuity, what are the income tax consequences if I die after I started taking distributions from it?*

Your plan's beneficiary will pay tax on the entire amount.

❖ Should I make my living trust the beneficiary of my annuity on my death?

This may or may not be a good idea. Under certain circumstances, a beneficiary may be able to extend the period of time over which annuity payments are made. This benefit is lost when a trust is the beneficiary of an annuity. The law says your trustee will have to take all of your annuity's taxable value into income within five years of your death.

However, if you need to have your trustee control the value of your annuity because of other considerations, such as a spendthrift beneficiary, making your trust the beneficiary would outweigh the shorter-time-period tax consideration.

❖ Is the entire value of my annuity included in my estate if I die during the accumulation period?

Yes; if you die during the accumulation period, the total value of your annuity will be included in your estate for federal estate tax purposes, whether you or your IRA owned the annuity.

❖ Does my estate have to pay estate tax on my annuity if I die after receiving payments from it?

If you begin annuitizing your annuity and die without a death benefit option, there will be no further payments from the company; and, of course, nothing will be included in your estate.

However, if you elected a survivor option so that payments continue to be made to your beneficiary, the value will be included in your estate, regardless of whether you or your IRA owned the annuity.

❖ **What if I elected a period certain to receive payments for ten years, and I only receive five years of payments before my death?**

The remaining five payments will be included in your estate.

❖ **What if I purchased a joint-and-survivor annuity for my spouse and me, and I die before my spouse?**

The law says that your estate will be charged with the amount the insurance company would charge your spouse to purchase a single-life annuity at the time of your death. However, because of the unlimited marital deduction, there will be no tax; so this is effectively a moot point, regardless of whether you or your IRA owned the annuity.

❖ **Do I have to pay federal gift tax if I give my annuity away?**

Yes, you do, regardless of whether you or your IRA owned the annuity.

❖ **If I purchase an annuity and immediately give it away, what is the value of my gift for gift tax purposes?**

Its value for gift tax purposes is the premium you or your IRA paid.

❖ **What if I or my IRA hold my annuity for a period of time and then make a gift of it?**

Calculating the value of your gift is more complicated. The gift is valued by ascertaining the single premium that the insurance company would charge for an annuity for a person the same age as you in the year of your gift.

❖ *How does the gift tax work?*

The answers are many and outside the purpose and scope of this book. However, if you will read our book, *How to Protect and Enhance Your Estate*, published by McGraw-Hill, you will quickly and easily learn the answer to your question.

Chapter Highlights

1. The principal of an annuity—your premium(s)—is not subject to income tax when you make withdrawals; unless the annuity is held in an IRA, 401(k) plan, or a company-sponsored qualified retirement plan.

2. All withdrawals from your IRA are income-taxed as ordinary income.

3. Other than annuities with income riders and a few other minor exceptions, each annuity payment you receive is partly tax-free return of principal and partly taxable income because of the exclusion ratio.

4. You or your IRA can exchange one annuity for another tax free under section 1035 of the Internal Revenue Code.

5. Gifts of annuities to others, including irrevocable trusts, are subject to federal gift taxation, and cause immediate taxation of all of the annuity's earnings. If the gift is of an IRA-owned annuity, it will cause immediate income-taxation of all of the annuity's proceeds.

6. Annuities that have a death benefit are included in the estates of their owners, and the beneficiaries will owe income taxes on any annuity earnings as the beneficiaries receive them.

· CHAPTER 10 ·

Commissions and Fees

In terms of the literature, this chapter could be reasonably and accurately entitled the *Nuclear Option*! Annuity antagonists "rage" in magazine articles, Internet blogs, and in popular investment books on what they consider to be the "outrageous" sales commissions and ongoing fees associated with fixed and indexed annuities. In response, insurance company executives, annuity advisors, and academic scholars shrug their shoulders and reply with: "What commissions and fees?"

Determining who's right and who's wrong with regard to this topically explosive issue is the task of this chapter.

❖ *Okay, let's start off with the bottom line: What are the commissions and administrative and maintenance fees associated with fixed and indexed annuities that I will pay if I buy one?*

There aren't any that you pay directly.

❖ *This is a chapter about commissions and fees, and you're saying they don't exist?*

Yes, *they do not exist*; at least as characterized by opponents of annuities!

❖ *How can that possibly be if so many articles and professionals are attacking them?*

All of an insurance company's costs in connection with building, distributing, and selling fixed and indexed annuities, along with the costs of administering and maintaining them, are taken into account when the insurance company prices its annuity products.

In common business language: They are priced on a "net-of-cost basis"; this means there are no additional costs to you, the consumer.

❖ *Can you give me another example of net-of-cost basis?*

Think about a bank's CDs and the charges and fees that you *don't* have to pay in purchasing a CD, because the bank has factored all of its costs—administrative, marketing, advertising, and sales costs—into setting the interest rate it gives you.

Life insurance companies do likewise. They take into consideration all of their costs when quoting your guaranteed annuity rate.

❖ *When you refer to all of their costs, what do you mean?*

As you consider buying a fixed or indexed annuity, you and your advisor will look at a variety of products and companies that provide them. You will compare the guaranteed rates, the ratings of the companies, the range of riders, and the suitability of the product for your circumstances. You will then decide which one or ones are better for you.

As long as you receive the products and benefits that you bargained for, then the internal costs of the insurance company offering them are absolutely irrelevant.

❖ Are you saying that the advisor who sells me an annuity doesn't receive a commission?

No, that is not what we are saying. We are saying that he or she receives a commission that is paid directly by the insurance company. When you purchase a fixed or indexed annuity, you do not pay a direct sales commission; because the company has absorbed its costs, including commissions, within the terms and conditions of the annuity contract it is offering you.

❖ But, I am paying a sales commission, because it is built in, right?

No; you are purchasing an annuity whose terms and conditions are set by the company after it has considered all of its costs—including marketing and sales costs—just like most other goods and services are delivered in our society. This principle applies to virtually all goods and services, including the fees professionals like us charge. An attorney's billing rate reflects the marketing costs of the law firm; and attorneys who bring in more business than others (called "rainmakers" in our jargon), are often billed and paid at higher rates than attorneys who do not bring in clients.

❖ So, do all of the articles reflect what you are saying?

Just the opposite. Most of them are highly critical about the high cost of annuities and talk about fees and administrative expenses in derogatory terms. Here are two examples of the headlines we have seen: "Buyer Beware" and "Indexed Annuities are a Safety Trap!"

❖ *How can these annuity antagonists be critical if the public doesn't pay direct commissions or fees on fixed or indexed annuities?*

We think the people who are writing negative articles can generally be lumped into a handful of categories:

- Well-meaning, but misinformed, pundits who are confusing fixed and indexed annuities with *variable* annuities. (You would be astounded, as we were, at how often this confusion cropped up in our research.)

- Thoughtful and well-informed pundits whose writings have valid criticisms that are levied against variable annuities, rather than fixed or indexed ones. They don't bother to explicitly point out that they are talking about annuities in general and not talking about fixed or indexed ones in their criticisms.

- Writers who are lumping the various crediting methodologies—such as participation, cap, and spread rates—into an administrative expense category, to which they do not belong.

- Writers who include the cost of purchasing riders as proof of additional sales charges, rather than for the purpose of buying additional benefits to the base annuity contracts.

❖ *Aren't you being a little harsh on these writers?*

We don't think so. You'll remember from your reading of chapter 1 on annuity basics that:

- Fixed and indexed annuities are *financial vehicles* focused on reducing the risk of losing your principal.

■ Variable annuities are *securities*—at-risk investments, very much like the stocks and bonds the variable annuities own—that fluctuate with the markets, without guarantees of any kind.

❖ *Are you saying that these writers don't know the difference?*

We have to believe that they must; which leads us to surmise that their writing skills are just not precise enough to explicitly point out that they are talking about variable products rather than guaranteed fixed and indexed ones.

❖ *What are the many costs and drawbacks of variable annuities?*

As we promised you in Chapter 1, The Mechanics of Annuity Basics, this *Guide* is not about variable annuities, and we are going to honor that promise.

❖ *Can you give me specific instances where writers confuse variable annuities with fixed and indexed annuities?*

We could give you countless ones, because it occurs everywhere in the literature. However, so as to not embarrass anyone, we encourage you to do your own research on the topic (online or otherwise) so that you can judge for yourself the confusion in the literature and what bloggers are incorrectly alleging in this area.

❖ **Can you address the allegations that there are additional administrative costs such as caps, spreads, and participation rates; and also surrender charges?**

We can. They are not sales costs, but simply cost factors built into your contract's performance that are absorbed by insurance companies through the pricing factors contained in your annuity contract.

❖ **Will there be additional costs if I want to add one or more riders to my contract?**

Yes; there likely will be additional charges for additional benefits, just like the automotive industry charges more for cars that have added features over their standard models.

As you will discover by reading the rest of this chapter—along with Chapter 6, Income Riders, and, Chapter 7, Long-Term-Care Riders—insurance companies are simply doing business as usual by charging for options that cost them more to provide.

❖ **Surely, you have to agree that advisors make commissions on riders?**

Yes; advisors may make commissions on some riders, but not on income riders. However, there is no way for you or us to know, because they are just built into the rates a company is willing to guarantee.

❖ **Can you cite an article where sales commissions and administrative costs are attacked?**

As we have said, they are ubiquitous. However, we believe it is in good taste and within our standards of professional conduct to cite, as but one example, an article that ran in *Money* magazine's January/February 2011 issue. It alleged, in part, that companies pay unusually high commissions to sales agents that lead to abuses in the sales process (and that's saying it nicely)[5].

In this case, the **National Association for Fixed Annuities (NAFA)** drafted a written response to the article. In studying this response, we determined it to be even-handed, and are comfortable quoting from it.

❖ *Before you do, what is NAFA's purpose?*

NAFA describes itself as:

> "The only association whose sole purpose is to educate regulators, legislators, consumers, members of the media, industry personnel, and distributors about fixed annuities (including indexed annuities) and their benefits to retirees and those planning for retirement."

❖ *So, they're a lobbying organization?*

In part, they certainly are; but that does not discredit the veracity of their response.

❖ *What was their response to the Money magazine article?*

First, they agreed that insurance companies pay sales commissions when annuities are sold, just like other financial products.

Second, they compared annuity commissions to commissions regularly received by securities advisors.

Third, they suggested that saying annuities are sold in a deceptive manner is, in-and-of-itself, deceptive.

❖ **What did they say about sales commissions?**

To quote a part of NAFA's lengthy and compelling response to the 2011 *Money* article:

> "But you should also consider: All financial vehicles have to cover the provider's sales and marketing expenses. Over time, the margins built into an annuity to cover commissions are not necessarily higher than the sales and marketing expense margins built into competing financial vehicles.
>
> Consider, for example the typical fee-based financial advisor. Such an advisor will often charge a fee of around 1% of assets annually, in addition to the expenses and fees built into the product itself. Now compare this to one of the best-selling indexed annuit[ies] in the marketplace, which gives agents...a choice of being paid a 7% commission in year 1, or a 2.25% commission in year 1 followed by a 1% annual trail commission. *The 7% commission is hardly egregious, as it is about the same as the present value of fees charged by security advisors.* (emphasis added)"[6]

❖ **What more did NAFA say about abusive and deceptive sales processes?**

They agreed with the *Money* article, that agents and advisors who are banned from the securities industry should, in most cases, be banned from the insurance industry as well; and vice versa. Basically, they stated the obvious: There are bad professionals in both industries. In our view, their response could be broadened to include every profession and industry—attorneys, accountants, physicians, financial advisors, etc.

They went on to say that state insurance regulators have a long history of protecting the public. You can glimpse the power of what NAFA is saying by reading some of the case studies in our Chapter 3, How Good Are Life Insurance Company Guarantees?

NAFA's response makes it clear that any consumer who has a problem with either an insurance company or an advisor selling an insurance product can enlist the help of their state's insurance department, because it: "…holds the power to assess fines, revoke licenses, and file criminal charges where needed without your having to submit to lengthy and costly mediation processes."

The lengthy and costly mediation processes NAFA's response refers to are those used almost exclusively by the securities industry when there are complaints.

❖ **Did they say anything more about comparing annuity sales practices to those in the securities industry?**

They did.

> "As a reporter in the financial press, you probably see reports of new Ponzi scheme convictions in the securities industry on seemingly a weekly basis. While investments are risky and subject to widely variable returns, indexed annuities, on the other hand, are safe financial products that provide returns that stay within a relatively narrow band—and that are guaranteed…"[7]

❖ **So, you are sticking with your assertion and belief that commissions and fees for fixed and indexed annuities are not paid directly by consumers like me?**

We are, and we are not the only professionals "sticking to this assertion."

The following is taken from a prestigious work by the Wharton Financial Institutions Center, entitled *Real World Index Annuity Returns*:

> "Unlike mutual funds, an FIA [fixed indexed annuity] does not deduct sales charges, management fees or 12b-1 marketing fees. Instead, the insurance company uses a small amount from the underlying portfolio which lowers participation in the market index to cover administrative costs and commissions to brokers.... Because the FIA provides policy crediting rate formulae and periodic annuity owner *reports net of any fees and management expenses, it does not separately disclose them.* (emphasis added)"[8]

Chapter Highlights

1. There are no commissions or administrative and maintenance fees associated with fixed and indexed annuities that are paid directly by you.

2. All of an insurance company's costs in connection with building, distributing, and selling fixed and indexed annuities, along with the costs of administering and maintaining them, are taken into account when the insurance company prices the annuity.

3. Critics who attack the high costs and commissions associated with annuities either confuse or fail to adequately explain the differences between variable annuities—which do have high costs and commissions—and fixed and indexed annuities that do not have them.

4. Commissions are not built into or paid on income riders.

·CHAPTER 11·

Is a Fixed or Indexed Annuity Suitable For You?

Most complaints, criticisms, and lawsuits arising out of the purchase of fixed and indexed annuities center on their being inappropriately sold to people who did not need them and should not have been induced to purchase them.

The industry term for this bad practice is "lack of **suitability**": whether a fixed or indexed annuity was suitable for you at the time you purchased it.

The regulatory authorities have addressed suitability by making insurance companies responsible for properly training annuity sellers, and have placed the major burden for determining suitability squarely on their shoulders.

This chapter does not dispute the responsibilities of either the companies or annuity advisors; rather, it addresses what we believe are *your responsibilities* in purchasing an annuity.

❖ *Who oversees the regulation of annuity sales?*

State insurance commissioners oversee how fixed and indexed annuities are sold, not the federal government or securities industry regulators.

❖ *Are insurance companies held accountable for suitability compliance as a result of their advisors selling their annuities?*

Yes. Insurance companies are being held accountable, and with ever-increasing and heightened suitability standards.

❖ *Are annuity sellers also being held to increasing suitability standards?*

Agents, financial advisors, brokers, and Registered Investment Advisors (RIAs) who sell annuities are being held to higher suitability standards.

Just because annuity sellers are held to these higher standards, however, does not, in our view, absolve you of taking some responsibility for making sure a fixed or indexed annuity is appropriate for you.

❖ *What are the basic areas of suitability information that I need to share with my annuity advisor?*

The National Association of Insurance Commissioners (NAIC) says that your annuity advisors need to obtain the following **suitability information** from you:

Suitability Information

YOUR AGE	Are you too young or too old to purchase an annuity?
YOUR TAX STATUS	Do your current and projected income tax rates justify the income tax benefits of fixed and indexed annuities?

Suitability Information, *cont'd*

THE INTENDED
PURPOSE

Are you buying an annuity to preserve your principal, achieve guarantees, or to generate a guaranteed income during your retirement years? If none of these reasons apply, are you buying it for reasons that have nothing to do with its intended purposes and benefits?

YOUR FINANCIAL TIME
HORIZON

When do you think you will need the money you are putting into the annuity? Are you putting money aside for later use, or will you need it in the near future?

YOUR EXISTING ASSETS

Are your existing assets sufficient to justify the percentage of them that you are putting into your annuity?

YOUR SOURCE OF FUNDS

Do you have bank savings or other liquid assets to purchase your annuity, or will you have to sell fixed assets at significant losses to generate the necessary premium? Are you selling any stocks, bonds, or mutual funds to purchase the annuity?

Suitability Information, *cont'd*

OTHER INSURANCE AND ANNUITY PRODUCTS

Do you have other insurance company products that would fit nicely with the recommended annuity, or would the recommended product be duplicative of or in conflict with your existing ones?

YOUR INVESTMENT OBJECTIVES

Are your objectives to protect and preserve your principal accompanied by modest, but guaranteed growth; or are you more comfortable speculating in stocks and bonds?

YOUR LIQUIDITY NEEDS

Do you have immediate or reasonably-anticipated short-term needs for your money (paying off a loan or buying a new home, etc.)?

YOUR LIQUID NET WORTH

If you purchase an annuity, will doing so unwisely deplete your cash reserves and force you to liquidate fixed assets?

YOUR TOLERANCE FOR RISK

How would you rate your risk tolerance on a scale of 1-10, with 1 meaning you do not wish to

Suitability Information, *cont'd*

risk your principal to any extent, and 10 being you will buy lottery tickets with it to gamble that you can hit the jackpot?

❖ *Would you suggest that I consider answering additional questions not posed by NAIC's list?*

We think you should also consider answering the following questions:

- Will you or your IRA own the annuity?

- How secure is your employment status?

- Will your immediate need for income remain constant?

- Do you have an emergency fund of six months expenses?

- Will your beneficiaries have access to liquid funds to carry on?

- Do you have medical problems your advisor should know about?

❖ *Does my advisor have additional requirements to determine that I pass muster on the suitability lists?*

Yes, NAIC says your advisor must have a "reasonable basis" to believe that you understand your annuity's basic features.

❖ *What do they mean by basic features?*

Basic features include contract provisions such as:

- Surrender charges

- Guaranteed interest rates

- Bonus interest rates

- Indexed rate crediting methods

- Tax-deferred growth

- Lifetime income riders

- Annuitization options

- Nursing home benefits

- Other living or death benefits

The state regulators say that each of these policy provisions must be explained and understood by you, and the burden for doing so is on the advisor.

❖ *This is a tall order! How can I help my advisor be comfortable that I have a basic understanding of these features?*

That is why you are reading this *Guide*. Your advisor gave it to you so that you could be better prepared to understand the specifics of your advisor's recommendations as you proceed through your annuity selection process.

❖ *Does my advisor have to keep records of what we talked about and the recommendations that the advisor made to me?*

NAIC requires advisors to retain records of any annuity recommendations that were made to you for a period between four and ten years, depending on your state's law.

❖ *Don't these added requirements mean that my advisor has to spend more time with me?*

Yes; and that's good news in our view, because you are likely to get counseling rather than a sales pitch. We think that these added regulatory requirements are doing what they were intended to accomplish: keeping irresponsible salespeople away from the public.

❖ *In general, what kind of people should consider fixed or indexed annuities?*

Kerry Pechter included a list of these people in her book, *Annuities for Dummies*.[9] We thought it was amusing and that it might be fun for you as well. Please note that in the following list, the categories on the left are Ms. Pechter's, but the explanations on the right are ours.

People	Reasons for Buying Annuities
BOOMER COUPLES WITH 401(K) AND 403(B) ACCOUNTS	Are middle-aged and have assets that fit readily into annuities

People, *cont'd*	**Reasons for Buying Annuities, *cont'd***
WOMEN	Will live longer than men, and will need income for more years
THE MIDDLE CLASS AND AFFLUENT FAMILIES	The assumption being they have money to put into annuities
RETIREES WHO DON'T HAVE A DEFINED BENE-FIT PENSION PLAN	These days, most everybody
PEOPLE WITH RUGGED GENES	A family history of longevity
MARKET BEARS AND OTHER PESSIMISTS	People who are afraid of losing their principal
NEITHER THE VERY YOUNG [N]OR THE VERY OLD	Young people don't need annuities. Really old people do not have enough years left to defer income, or even to take payouts because of their shortened life spans.
PEOPLE WHO WANT TO TURN A TAX BITE INTO BITE-SIZED PIECES	Take advantage of income tax deferral and the exclusion ratio after annuitization

People, *cont'd*	Reasons for Buying Annuities, *cont'd*
THOSE SEEKING LESS-EXPENSIVE LONG-TERM-CARE INSURANCE	(We disagree with her on this one, but include it out of discipline in sharing her list with you.)
PEOPLE WITHOUT BENEFICIARIES	Only care about maximizing their lifetime incomes

❖ *Do you have a list that's different from the one above?*

No; we would use different language, and perhaps discount a few items on this list, but otherwise believe it goes to the heart of the matter.

❖ *How do I know whether I am an unsuitable candidate for an annuity?*

You should be extra careful in making a fixed or indexed annuity decision if any of the following apply to you:

- Think you need access to your entire principal within five or maybe ten years.

- Don't have that many years left to live based on the actuarial tables.

- Have a low tax bracket and do not need tax deferral or the exclusion ratio.

- Think you will not gain that much added benefit from purchasing an annuity.

■ Are uncomfortable with your understanding of how annuities can benefit you.

❖ How much of my money do you think I should put into an annuity?

This is a difficult question to answer, because the authorities do not agree. It depends upon your goals and objectives, and your financial situation.

Some authorities, such as the author of a scholarly Wharton School white paper, believe that if you can determine your income needs, it is perfectly acceptable to fund an annuity with "up to 100 percent of your money." Other authorities vary in quoting percentages ranging from 30 to 100 percent.

In our view, you should only fund one or more annuities with money that you don't need for other purposes, especially in the short run. *Annuities are long-term products.*

❖ What if I'm considering replacing another annuity?

A significant percentage of annuity sales occur because of this; but understand that surrender charges that may be generated as a result. (There has been considerable criticism of advisors replacing annuities just to receive the sales commissions, because of this surrender charge possibility.)

However, there are a number of good reasons for replacing existing annuities that begin and end with mathematics. Here are two questions you should ask:

■ Does the recommended annuity make me more or less money than my existing annuity after considering the cost of surrender charges, if any?

- Can I get a written comparison that I can study and retain, especially if things do not turn out the way I expected them to?

❖ *If I purchase an annuity, can I change my mind?*

Yes, you will have a thirty-day **free-look period**. If you change your mind during that period, you can return your annuity and receive a full refund.

❖ *What do you recommend I do during that period?*

If you have any questions or concerns that your annuity advisor did not satisfactorily address, we would suggest that you call the toll-free telephone number on the top of your annuity statement and ask your questions, or address your concerns directly with the proper company authority.

Chapter Highlights

1. You should only buy an annuity if it is suitable for you.

2. The burden of determining if an annuity is suitable for you is primarily on the advisor who sells the annuity to you, but we feel strongly that you have a responsibility to participate fully and honestly in the suitability discussions.

3. Suitability is based on a number of financial and personal factors that ensure that you have the need for an annuity as a part of your overall planning.

4. You should expend the time to make sure that you have a fundamental understanding of the basic features of the annuity that you intend to purchase and how it will benefit you.

CHAPTER 12

The Alleged Benefits of Fixed Annuities

Fixed annuity advocates identify a number of core issues in making their case for their use.

Like a trial judge, we have read and studied their arguments extolling their virtues; and after considerable discussion and deliberation, have arrived at our conclusions.

This chapter provides you with our judgments on the claims made specifically by fixed annuity advocates in support of their efficacy.

Proponents' Claim	Our Judgment

POPULARITY

Fixed annuities are gaining in popularity.

Reported company statistics and newsworthy reports make clear that fixed annuities are solidly holding their own in the marketplace, but that they are not "booming" to the extent of their indexed annuity cousins.

SAFETY

A fixed annuity's principal and the income it earns are safe.

We believe a fixed annuity is far safer than any competing investment opportunity that is

Proponents' Claim, *cont'd*	**Our Judgment,** *cont'd*
	subject to fluctuating market risks and steep downturns, whether in stocks or bonds. (Remember, fixed annuities are not investments.)

We also believe—with one qualification—that a fixed annuity is almost as secure with a quality insurance company as the FDIC-insured bank savings alternative.

Our one qualification is that you put your money with a life insurance company that has an "A" in its rating with each of the four rating agencies, and a 75 or greater COMDEX rating.

PAYMENTS FOR LIFE

A fixed annuity will pay you for your entire lifetime, regardless of how long you live.

True; it will when you annuitize it. Income for life is an essential annuity benefit.

STRESS

A fixed annuity is hassle free.

It is. You will not have to follow the equity or bond markets, be

Proponents' Claim, cont'd	**Our Judgment, cont'd**
	concerned with the performance of your money manager or financial advisor, or react to precipitous market collapses.

COMPOUND INTEREST

Fixed annuities get the benefit of compound interest.	They generally do. Some products may not offer compound interest, though, so make sure that your fixed annuity does.

DEFERRED TAXATION

A fixed annuity guarantees deferred income tax advantages.	True. If you own your annuity outside of an IRA, it will grow and compound without your having to pay annual income taxes on that growth during its accumulation period. This is a major benefit that you do not enjoy with other financial vehicles you own outside of an IRA. If your IRA owns the annuity, it will also grow and compound without your having to pay annual income taxes on that growth as is the case with all IRA-owned assets.

Proponents' Claim, *cont'd*	**Our Judgment,** *cont'd*

BENEFICIAL TAXATION ON RECEIPT

A fixed annuity provides you with additional income tax advantages when you begin receiving payments.

True. If you own the annuity outside of an IRA, you will receive the benefit of the exclusion ratio during the annuitization period, and pay income taxes only on a portion of your annuity payments for your entire life expectancy. Other savings vehicles do not enjoy this privilege. However, there is no additional income tax benefit or detriment if your IRA owns the annuity.

BETTER THAN CDs

A fixed annuity compounds better than a CD.

True. If you own your annuity outside of an IRA, the annuity will compound on a tax-deferred basis, which does not happen with a CD. If your IRA owns the annuity and the CDs, both are income-tax-deferred.

Regardless of the tax deferral consideration, the literature and historical studies clearly show that your fixed annuity is likely to do 1 to 2 percent better

Proponents' Claim, cont'd	**Our Judgment, cont'd**
	each year than competing bank savings products, and will be even more competitive over longer terms.

INFLATION

A fixed annuity keeps pace with inflation.

Probably not. It will do a better job than CDs, but may not do as well as some at-risk portfolios.

COSTS

You do not pay up-front management and administrative fees and sales commissions.

True; management and administrative expenses, along with selling commissions, are paid solely by companies as internal company expenses.

INTEREST SENSITIVE

A fixed annuity keeps pace with interest rates if they go up.

True, the company will adjust your interest rate annually to market conditions in order to be competitive with savings institutions.

ACCESS TO PRINCIPAL

A fixed annuity provides you with flexible and affordable opportunities to withdraw principal if and when you need it.

True and not true. It does so over the long term, but generally not so much within the first five to seven years of your contract,

Proponents' Claim, *cont'd*	**Our Judgment,** *cont'd*
	because of early withdrawal charges. If it is your expectation that you will need immediate access to your funds, you should consider other planning alternatives.

ADDITIONAL INCOME

You can purchase an income rider to provide additional income during your lifetime.	Not true in our experience. Income riders are most always purchased with indexed annuities, but not with fixed ones.

HELPING FAMILY MEMBERS

A fixed annuity allows you to continue payments to your beneficiaries after your death?	True. There are a number of long-standing options for you to do so.

CREDITOR PROTECTION ON DEATH

A fixed annuity avoids the claims of creditors on death.	True. It will.

NO PROBATE ON DEATH

A fixed annuity automatically avoids probate on death.	True, so long as the estate is not named as beneficiary.

Proponents' Claim, cont'd	**Our Judgment, cont'd**

LIFETIME CREDITOR PROTECTION

A fixed annuity avoids the claims of creditors while you are alive.

It will fully do so in some states, partially in others, but not at all in a minority of others—it depends upon the laws of your home state: You will need to check with your annuity advisor to determine your state's law.

EASE OF REDRESS

You can easily assert your rights if you have difficultieswith either the company or the advisor who sold it to you.

True. You can file a complaint with your state's insurance department. It will investigate your complaint, and take whatever action is appropriate without your having to go to the legal expense of arbitration or trial—the remedies that are common to controversies with at-risk investment entities and advisors.

TRANSFERRING BETWEEN ANNUITIES

You can transfer a fixed annuity to another fixed annuity without having to suffer penalties for doing so.

True. You can do so through an income-tax-free section 1035 exchange. You may also avoid surrender charges if the transfer is within the same company.

Proponents' Claim, *cont'd*	Our Judgment, *cont'd*

Your IRA may also do so under retirement law.

AVOIDING RMD WORRIES

You do not have to worry about required minimum distributions after you roll over your IRA into an annuity.	Not true. There is a 50 percent tax penalty for not making RMDs. Most companies automatically monitor minimum distribution requirements for you without legal or accounting charges to make sure you won't have to pay that penalty.

MARKET CONSENSUS

Most people are happy with their fixed annuities.	True. We have not discovered credible studies or evidence to the contrary.

Chapter Highlights

1. Fixed annuities have not been subjected to the degree of criticism that has been levied against their indexed cousins.

2. There are a great many benefits and reasons for using fixed annuities that every advisor and potential annuity purchaser should be aware of.

3. Fixed annuities are not investments. They are long-term financial vehicles and should only be used for that purpose.

4. When used properly, fixed annuities can be an effective method to meet a person's financial goals.

CHAPTER 13

The Alleged Detriments of Fixed Annuities

Fixed annuity critics identify a number of core issues in making their case that fixed annuities should be avoided in favor of other "investment" opportunities and strategies.

Like a trial judge, we have read and studied their arguments; and after considerable discussion and deliberation, have arrived at our conclusions.

This chapter provides you with our judgments on the "alleged" claims made by fixed annuity naysayers.

Critics' Claim	Our Judgment

TOO COMPLEX

Fixed annuities are overly complex.

True, they are; but not as complex as indexed annuities.

DECEPTIVE SALES PRACTICES

Fixed annuities are sold in a deceptive manner.

We have done a significant amount of research on this allegation, and believe it is without empirical foundation,

Critics' Claim, *cont'd*	Our Judgment, *cont'd*
	and vastly incorrect. Using the adjective "deceptive" is too strong, patently unfair, and without substantiation other than in a very few reported cases. It is our further judgment that a number of advisors criticize them purely out of a stocks-and bonds-based bias. And that other unsophisticated advisors who do not specialize in annuities over-simplify or skirt important technical considerations in their critiques out of ignorance; rather than out of chicanery or malice.

INAPPROPRIATE SELLING

Fixed annuities are sold inappropriately to inappropriate people.	It is true that some advisors do sell fixed annuities inappropriately to inappropriate people, just as attorneys and doctors malpractice, and investment advisors make inappropriate investment recommendations. However, we were able to find relatively few complaints levied against advisors for inappropriately selling fixed annuities.

Critics' Claim, *cont'd*	Our Judgment, *cont'd*

COMMISSION FOCUSED

Annuity advisors mainly sell the fixed annuity products that will make them the most money, rather than the ones that will best fit their clients' needs.

Not true, in the main. Annuity advisors, like all professionals, do the right thing by their clients. However, there are surely bad apples selling annuities just as there are bad apples selling stocks and bonds—or for that matter, selling anything else.

LACK OF TRAINING

Advisors don't have to pass examinations to be licensed to sell fixed annuities.

Not true. They have to pass an examination to be licensed by the state, just as advisors who sell stocks and bonds have to pass one or more examinations to sell securities and other financial products.

LACK OF REGULATION

Fixed annuities are unregulated compared to securities.

True and not true. The fixed annuity industry and its advisors are not regulated by the Financial Industry Regulatory Authority (FINRA)—a non-governmental authority—or by the federal Securities and Exchange Commission (SEC). Instead, they are regulated by state insurance departments.

Critics' Claim, *cont'd*	Our Judgment, *cont'd*
	Whether this is a "negative" or a "positive" is conjectural at best; and the topic of a raging debate between the annuity and equity industries, that makes little substantive sense to us.

MALAISE IN ENFORCEMENT

Insurance commissioners haven't really worked to clean up industry abuses.	Not true. Based on our research and the work of NAFA, the record shows increasing efforts for consumer protection in recent years.

HISTORY OF COMPANY FAILURES

People who purchase fixed annuities risk their principal due to repeated insurance company failures, and the likelihood it could happen to their companies.	Not true. We covered this on the "benefits" side of the ledger, and are convinced that this criticism is theoretical and without practical merit, so long as purchasers select highly rated companies.

REDUNDANT BENEFITS

The tax-deferral benefit of a fixed annuity is redundant if it is in an IRA.	That is true. But, it should be noted that only approximately 50 percent of buyers are

Critics' Claim, *cont'd*	Our Judgment, *cont'd*

IRAs, and that there are other, more significant reasons—like protecting your principal—that must be considered in assessing whether or not your IRA should own one.

NO CAPITAL GAINS

Fixed annuity payments are not taxed at preferential capital gains rates like stocks.

This is true, because only investment assets are categorized as capital assets. Fixed annuities are not investment assets. They enjoy tax-deferred status during the accumulation period, and preferential exclusion ratio treatment during their annuitization period.

BAD SURRENDER PENALTIES

Fixed annuity surrender penalties are onerous in both duration and amount.

True and not true, depending upon your time perspective: Annuities are designed for long-term holding periods to benefit both their purchasers' needs, and those of the companies issuing them. They are not designed for short-term use.

Surrender charges are reflected in seven- to ten-year schedules so that companies can invest the money, and make money to cover their up-front costs.

Critics' Claim, *cont'd*	Our Judgment, *cont'd*

10 PERCENT TAX PENALTY

Withdrawals from fixed annuities before age 59½ are subject to a 10 percent income tax penalty.

True and not true. Critics imply that the penalty is on all withdrawals. The truth is they are only on withdrawals of earnings.

Critics also imply that there are no exceptions to this penalty tax, but there are: Withdrawals made pursuant to an approved systematic plan are exempt.

This is true for withdrawals from your IRA-owned annuity as well.

ADMINISTRATIVE FEES

Administrative fees eat into fixed annuity returns.

Not true; they are absorbed by the company as part of the cost of providing the annuity.

POOR PERFORMANCE

The performance of fixed annuities is considerably below the performance expected by directly investing in various stock, bond, or commodity indexes.

This is not a valid comparison: Your fixed annuity's principal is company-insured, whereas your direct investments are at-risk investments that could go way up or plummet in volatile markets.

Critics' Claim, *cont'd*	Our Judgment, *cont'd*

BONUS COME-ON

Up-front bonuses are of no real value and just a "come-on" for people to buy fixed annuities, or to switch their existing ones to other companies.

True and not true. A fixed annuity that has an up-front bonus on purchase will have lower declared rate than annuities without a bonus. However, if you keep your money in your annuity past the surrender charge period, the bonus will be of significant value to you.

LACK OF DIVERSIFICATION

People would be better off investing in diversified portfolios rather than limiting themselves to just fixed annuities.

Not true; you purchase a fixed annuity to reduce the risk of losing your principal. A diversified portfolio of at-risk investments does not guarantee the safety of your principal.

(In an aside, however, this statement reminds us of a client, a magnate in the technology industry, who was encouraged by his advisors to liquidate his industry holdings to diversify into real estate and bank stocks in his native State of Texas. After doing so he lost a fortune—50 percent of his money—while the industry stocks he sold doubled in value.)

Critics' Claim, *cont'd*	Our Judgment, *cont'd*

PREMIUM TAXES

States assess taxes on annuity premiums.

Forty-four states do not assess any taxes, and six states assess minor taxes that are generally paid by the issuing companies.

ONEROUS COSTS

The costs of annuities are not worth the minimal return I'll get over government-backed CDs.

This criticism is fallacious. Your annuity's returns are net of its costs.

Chapter Highlights

1. Fixed annuities have been criticized for their lack of "investment" potential. Fixed annuities are not investments. They are long-term financial vehicles and should only be critiqued with that purpose in mind.

2. There are a great many allegations against the use of fixed annuities, some of which every advisor and potential annuity purchaser should be aware of.

3. Most all of the allegations against them have been hollow or unsubstantiated.

4. When used properly, fixed annuities can be an effective method to meet a person's financial goals.

CHAPTER 14

The Alleged Benefits of Indexed Annuities

This chapter is largely redundant to Chapter 12, The Alleged Benefits of Fixed Annuities, but we keep the chapters separate because there are meaningful differences between fixed and indexed annuities, and how they are lauded by their proponents.

Indexed annuity advocates identify a number of core issues in making their case for their use.

Like a trial judge, we have read and studied their arguments extolling their virtues; and after considerable discussion and deliberation, have arrived at our conclusions.

This chapter provides you with our judgments on the claims made specifically by advocates of indexed annuities supporting their efficacy.

Proponents' Claim	Our Judgment

POPULARITY

Indexed annuities are gaining in popularity.

Reported company statistics and newsworthy reports make clear that indexed annuities are "booming," or at least steadily gaining in popularity given mounting fears of market volatility in unprecedented economic times since 2008.

Proponents' Claim, *cont'd*	**Our Judgment,** *cont'd*

SAFETY

An indexed annuity's principal and the income it earns are safer than investments.

We believe an indexed annuity is far safer than any investment that is subject to fluctuating market risks and steep downturns. (Remember, indexed annuities are not investments.)

We also believe—with one qualification—that an indexed annuity is almost as protected with a quality insurance company as an FDIC-insured bank savings alternative.

Our one qualification is that you purchase an annuity from a life insurance company that has an "A" in its rating with each of the four rating agencies, and a 75 or greater COMDEX rating.

UPSIDE WITH NO DOWNSIDE

An indexed annuity gets a portion of upside gains in the stock market without risking anything in declining or collapsing markets.

We agree. This feature is the bulwark justification for indexed annuities.

Proponents' Claim, *cont'd*	**Our Judgment,** *cont'd*

PAYMENTS FOR LIFE

An indexed annuity will pay you for your entire lifetime, regardless of how long you live

True, it will when you annuitize it, or purchase an income rider. Income for life is an essential annuity benefit.

STRESS

An indexed annuity is hasle-free.

It is. You will not have to follow the equity or bond markets, be concerned with the performance of your money manager or financial advisor, or react to precipitous market collapses.

COMPOUND INTEREST

Indexed annuities get the benefit of compound interest.

They generally do. Some products may not offer compound interest, though, so make sure that your annuity does.

DEFERRED TAXATION

An indexed annuity guarantees deferred income tax advantages.

True. If you own your annuity outside of an IRA, it will grow and compound without your having to pay annual income taxes on that growth during its accumulation period. This

Proponents' Claim, *cont'd*	Our Judgment, *cont'd*
	is a major benefit that you do not enjoy with other financial vehicles you own outside of an IRA. If your IRA owns the annuity, it will also grow and compound without your having to pay annual income taxes on that growth, as is the case with all IRA-owned assets.

BENEFICIAL TAXATION ON RECEIPT

An indexed annuity provides you with additional income tax advantages when you begin receiving payments.

True. If you own the annuity outside of an IRA, you will receive the benefit of the exclusion ratio during the annuitization period, and pay income taxes only on a portion of your annuity payments for your entire life expectancy. Other vehicles do not enjoy this privilege. However, there is no additional income tax benefit or detriment if your IRA owns the annuity.

BETTER THAN CDS

An indexed annuity compounds better than a CD.

True. If you own your annuity outside of an IRA, the annuity will compound on a tax-deferred

Proponents' Claim, *cont'd*	**Our Judgment,** *cont'd*

basis, which does not happen with a CD. If your IRA owns the annuity and the CDs, both are income-tax-deferred.

Regardless of the tax deferral consideration, the literature and historical studies clearly show that your indexed annuity is likely to do 1 to 2 percent better each year than competing bank savings products, and will be even more competitive over longer terms.

COMPETITIVE GROWTH

An indexed annuity's growth is competitive with a portflio of stocks and bonds.

We cannot reach a judgment on this question, given the lack of situational facts.

However, an objective study by the highly respected Wharton Center of Personal Finance reached the conclusion that indexed annuities have been competitive with stocks and bonds when actual performance is measured, rather than theoretical performance based on mathematical models using assumed rates of return.

Proponents' Claim, cont'd	Our Judgment, cont'd
	In looking to other comparative studies, we could not reach an objective decision, because they appeared flawed as either being without academic credentials, using poorly documented substantiation, or were based on what we perceived to be the obvious bias of their authors.

BETTER THAN FIXED ANNUITIES

The indexing feature will likely give a greater return than a fixed annuity.	True, but the difference may not be as great as some of its proponents boast.

INFLATION

An indexed annuity keeps pace with inflation.	It will do better than CDs and fixed annuities, but may not do as well as some at-risk portfolios.

COSTS

You do not pay up-front management and administrative fees and sales commissions.	True. Management and administrative expenses, along with selling commissions, are paid solely by companies as internal company expenses.

Proponents' Claim, cont'd	**Our Judgment, cont'd**

INTEREST SENSITIVE

An indexed annuity keeps pace with interest rates if they go up.

True. The company will adjust your interest rate annually to market conditions in order to be competitive with savings institutions.

ACCESS TO PRINCIPAL

An indexed annuity provides you with flexible and affordable opportunities to withdraw principal if and when you need it.

True and not true. It does so over the long term, but generally not so much within the first five to seven years of your contract, because of early withdrawal charges. If it is your expectation that you will need immediate access to your funds, you should consider other planning alternatives.

ADDITIONAL INCOME

You can purchase an income rider to provide additional income during your lifetime.

True; you can. However, you must determine whether this rider fits your planning needs relative to its cost, which is around 1 percent per year.

HELPING FAMILY MEMBERS

An indexed annuity allows you to continue payments to your beneficiaries after your death.

True. There are a number of long-standing options for you to do so.

Proponents' Claim, cont'd	Our Judgment, cont'd

CREDITOR PROTECTION ON DEATH

An indexed annuity avoids the claims of creditors on death.

True. It will do so.

NO PROBATE ON DEATH

An indexed annuity automatically avoids probate on death.

True, so long as the estate is not named as beneficiary.

LIFETIME CREDITOR PROTECTION

An indexed annuity avoids the claims of your creditors while you are alive.

It will fully do so in some states, partially in others, but not at all in a minority of others—it depends upon the laws of your home state: You will need to check with your annuity advisor to determine your state's law.

EASE OF REDRESS

You can easily assert your rights if you have difficulties with either the company or the advisor who sold it to you.

True. You can file a complaint with your state's insurance department. It will investigate your complaint, and take whatever action is appropriate without your having to go to the expense of arbitration or trial—

Proponents' Claim, cont'd	**Our Judgment, cont'd**
	the remedies that are common to controversies with at-risk investment entities and advisors.

TRANSFERRING BETWEEN ANNUITIES

You can transfer an indexed annuity to another indexed annuity without having to suffer penalties for doing so.	True. You can do so through an income-tax-free section 1035 exchange. You may also avoid surrender charges if the transfer is within the same company. Your IRA may also do so under retirement law.

AVOIDING RMD WORRIES

You do not have to worry about required minimum distributions after you roll over your IRA into your annuity.	Not true. There is a 50 percent tax penalty for not making RMDs. Most companies automatically monitor minimum distribution requirements for you without legal or accounting charges to make sure you won't have to pay that penalty.

MARKET CONSENSUS

Most people are happy with their indexed annuities.	True. We have not discovered credible studies or evidence to the contrary.

Chapter Highlights

1. Indexed annuities have been subject to a debate as to their effectiveness since their inception.

2. There are a great many benefits and reasons for using indexed annuities that every advisor and potential annuity purchaser should be aware of.

3. Indexed annuities are not investments. They are long-term financial vehicles and should only be used for that purpose.

4. When used properly, an indexed annuity can be an effective method to meet a person's financial goals.

CHAPTER 15

The Alleged Detriments of Indexed Annuities

This chapter is largely redundant to Chapter 13, The Alleged Detriments of Fixed Annuities, but we keep them separate chapters because there are meaningful differences between fixed and indexed annuities, and how they are criticized by their detractors.

Indexed annuity critics identify a number of core issues in making their case that indexed annuities should be avoided in favor of other "investment" opportunities and strategies.

Like a trial judge, we have read and studied their arguments; and after considerable discussion and deliberation, have arrived at our conclusions.

This chapter provides you with our judgments on the "alleged" claims made specifically by indexed annuity naysayers.

Critics' Claim	Our Judgment

TOO COMPLEX

Indexed annuities are overly complex.	This is a valid criticism. Companies have been forced to compete with each other to curry favor with advisors and the public. To do so, they have continually been inventing

Critics' Claim, *cont'd*	Our Judgment, *cont'd*

new products, buzz words, and "bells and whistles" to differentiate themselves in the marketplace. In the end, all of their machinations end with about the same results in terms of the returns they will provide to their owners.

As the guardian of the fixed and indexed annuity industry, NAFA defends the complexity of indexed annuities with the comparison to Henry Ford's losing assertion that "You can have any color you want, so long as it is black." It is NAFA's position that many choices are good for consumers, even though they may not result in markedly different over-all benefits. And given their obvious popularity, we find it difficult to disagree.

DECEPTIVE SALES PRACTICES

Indexed annuities are sold in a deceptive manner.

Using the "deceptive" adjective is too strong, patently unfair, and without substantiation other than in a few reported egregious cases.

Rather, it is our judgment that a number of unsophisticated

Critics' Claim, *cont'd*	Our Judgment, *cont'd*
	advisors who do not specialize in annuities over-simplify or skirt important technical considerations out of ignorance, rather than out of chicanery or malice.

INAPPROPRIATE SELLING

Indexed annuities are sold inappropriately to inappropriate people.	It is true that some advisors do sell indexed annuities inappropriately to inappropriate people, just as some attorneys and doctors malpractice; and some investment advisors make inappropriate investment recommendations. However, we were able to find relatively few complaints levied against advisors for inappropriately selling indexed annuities.

COMMISSION FOCUSED

Annuity advisors mainly sell the indexed annuity products that will make them the most money, rather than the ones that will best fit their clients' needs.	Not true, in the main. Annuity advisors, like all professionals, do the right thing by their clients. However, there are surely bad apples selling annuities just as there are bad apples selling stocks and bonds—or for that matter, selling anything else.

Critics' Claim, *cont'd*	Our Judgment, *cont'd*

LACK OF TRAINING

Advisors don't have to pass examinations to be licensed to sell indexed annuities.

Not true. They have to pass an examination to be licensed by the state, just as advisors who sell stocks and bonds have to pass one or more examinations to sell securities and other financial products.

LACK OF REGULATION

Indexed annuities are unregulated compared to securities.

True and not true. The indexed annuity industry and its advisors are not regulated by the Financial Industry Regulatory Authority (FINRA)—a non-governmental authority—or by the federal Securities and Exchange Commission (SEC). Instead, they are regulated by state insurance departments.

Whether this is a "positive" or a "negative" is conjectural at best; and is the topic of a raging territorial debate between the annuity and equity industries, that makes little substantive sense to us.

Critics' Claim, *cont'd*	Our Judgment, *cont'd*

MALAISE IN ENFORCEMENT

Insurance commissioners have not really worked to clean up industry abuses.

Not true. Based on our research and the work of NAIC, the record shows increasing efforts for consumer protection in recent years.

HISTORY OF COMPANY FAILURES

People who purchase indexed annuities risk their principal due to repeated insurance company failures, and the likelihood it could happen to their companies.

Not true. We covered this on the "benefits" side of the ledger, and are convinced that this criticism is theoretical and without practical merit, so long as purchasers select highly rated companies.

REDUNDANT BENEFITS

The tax-deferral benefit of an indexed annuity is redundant if it is in an IRA.

This is true. But, it should be noted that approximately 50 percent of buyers are IRA buyers, and that there are other, more significant reasons—like protecting your principal—that must be considered in assessing whether or not your IRA should own one.

Critics' Claim, *cont'd*	Our Judgment, *cont'd*

NO CAPITAL GAINS

Indexed annuity payments are not taxed at preferential capital gains rates like stocks.

This is true, because only investment assets are categorized as capital assets. Indexed annuities are not investment assets. They enjoy tax-deferred status during the accumulation period, and preferential exclusion ratio treatment during their annuitization period.

BAD SURRENDER PENALTIES

Indexed annuity surrender penalties are onerous in both duration and amount.

True and not true, depending on your time perspective: Annuities are designed for long-term holding periods to benefit both their purchasers' needs, and those of the companies issuing them. They are not designed for short-term use.

Surrender charges are reflected in seven to ten-year schedules so that companies can invest the money, and make money to cover their up-front costs.

10 PERCENT TAX PENALTY

Withdrawals from indexed annuities before age 59½ are subject to a 10 percent income tax penalty.

True and not true. Critics imply that the penalty is on all withdrawals. The truth is they are only on withdrawals of earnings.

Critics' Claim, *cont'd*	Our Judgment, *cont'd*
	Critics also imply that there are no exceptions to this penalty tax, but there are—withdrawals made pursuant to an approved systematic plan are exempt.
	This is true for withdrawals from your IRA-owned annuity as well.

ADMINISTRATIVE FEES

Administrative fees eat into indexed annuity returns.	Not true; they are absorbed by the company as part of the cost of providing the annuity.

POOR PERFORMANCE

The performance of indexed annuities is considerably below the performance expected by directly investing in various stock, bond, or commodity indexes.	This is not a valid comparison. Your indexed annuity's principal is company-insured, whereas your direct investments are at-risk investments that could go way up or plummet in volatile markets.

SUPPRESSED GROWTH OPPORTUNITY

Companies use participation rates, caps, and spreads to limit the opportunity for gains in indexed annuities.	This is absolutely true. For them to do otherwise would bankrupt them, and your annuity as well.

Critics' Claim, *cont'd*	Our Judgment, *cont'd*

BONUS COME–ON

Up-front bonuses are of no real value and just a "come-on" for people to buy indexed annuities, or to switch their existing ones to other companies.

True and not true. An indexed annuity that has an up-front bonus on purchase will have lower participation rates and lower caps than annuities without a bonus. However, if you keep your money in your annuity past the surrender charge period, the bonus will likely result in more interest being credited to your annuity.

INCOME RIDER INFERIORITY

The features of an income rider are inferior to an immediate annuity.

True and not true. If you need income immediately, you would be better off with a SPIA. However, if your income need is for retirement ten years or more in the future, an income rider might be better suited to your needs.

LACK OF DIVERSIFICATION

People would be better off investing in diversified portfolios rather than limit themselves to just indexed annuities.

Not true; you purchase an indexed annuity to reduce the risk of losing your principal. A diversified portfolio of at-risk investments does not guarantee the safety of your principal.

Critics' Claim, *cont'd*	**Our Judgment,** *cont'd*

(An an aside, however, your question reminds us of a client, a magnate in the technology industry, who was encouraged by his advisors to liquidate his industry holdings to diversify into real estate and bank stocks in his native State of Texas. After doing so he lost a fortune—50 percent of his money—while the industry stocks he sold doubled in value.)

PREMIUM TAXES

States assess taxes on annuity premiums.

Forty-four states do not assess any taxes, and six states assess minor taxes that are generally paid by the issuing companies.

ONEROUS COSTS

The costs of annuities are not worth the minimal return I'll get over government-backed CDs

This criticism is fallacious. Your annuity's returns are net of its costs.

DIVIDENDS EXCLUDED

Indexed annuities exclude dividends on the indexes they refer to.

True, they exclude dividends. However, this alleged negative is like comparing football to badminton; it is simply not relevant, and is of no consequence in making a reasonable comparison.

Chapter Highlights

1. Indexed annuities have been subject to a debate as to their "investment" effectiveness. Indexed annuities are not investments. They are long-term financial vehicles, and should only be critiqued with that purpose in mind.

2. There are a many allegations against the use of indexed annuities, some of which every advisor and potential annuity purchaser should be aware of.

3. Most of the allegations against them have been hollow or unsubstantiated.

4. When used properly, indexed annuities can be an effective method to meet a person's financial goals.

·CHAPTER 16·

Highlights and Insights

There can be no question that some elements of indexed and fixed annuities are easily explained and understood, while others are dauntingly difficult.

Throughout this *Guide* we have tried our best to go deep enough into the technicalities so as not to mislead you by saying too little or too much; and to heighten your understanding by using non-technical language.

In reviewing our work, we realized we had particular thoughts that we think of as "insights" that might help you fit the various pieces of the fixed and indexed annuity puzzle together into a recognized and understandable picture.

As such, in this chapter we share the *Highlights* of each of the previous chapters juxtaposed with our *Insights* and *Judgments* in the hope that doing so will be helpful to you.

CHAPTER 1
———————— The Mechanics of Annuity Basics ————————

Highlights

1. A commercial annuity is a contract with a life insurance company, in which you give the company money—usually in a lump sum—in exchange for the company'spromise to give it back to you over a period of time with added interest or in some cases, any appreciation in value of the principal.

2. The "big three" annuity types are variable, fixed, and indexed.

3. Variable annuities are considered a publicly-traded security, such as a stock and bond, and subject to market risk; and are not the subject of this *Guide*.

4. In fixed annuities, a life insurance company promises to guarantee the return of your principal and pay you a guaranteed rate of interest.

5. Indexed annuities are like fixed annuities, except that the insurance company guarantees a maximum percentage or amount that your principal can go up based upon the performance of the stock market indexes, somewhat like a variable annuity, but without the same investment risks.

Insights

DEFERRED ANNUITIES

Fixed and indexed are deferred annuities that grow during an accumulation period, and provide you with money during the payout period you select.

PROTECTING PRINCIPAL

The crucial reason to purchase a fixed or indexed annuity is to protect your principal.

COMPANY GUARANTEES

Annuities are guaranteed by the issuing insurance companies; they are not investments.

INDEXED ANNUITIES

Indexed annuities are like fixed annuities except they are linked to stock indexes to give you the potential of greater earnings.

CHAPTER 2

——— Comparing Annuities to Bank Certificates ———
of Deposit

Highlights

1. Do not rely on basic charts or articles when comparing annuities and CDs; they are often gross generalizations or incorrect.

2. Annuities owned outside of IRAs compound interest on a tax-deferred basis, giving them a significant advantage over CDs that are owned outside of IRAs.

3. Annuities will generally pay a greater rate of return than CDs, because of the features they contain and their ability to defer income taxes.

4. CDs are protected by the FDIC. Annuities are protected by life insurance company guarantees; and some states have additional protections for annuities.

5. Both CDs and annuities are subject to delivery and distribution costs and related expenses, so it is incorrect to state that CDs do not have sales commissions and annuities do.

6. Both CDs and annuities have penalties for early withdrawals, but annuities have exceptions to penalties that allow annuity owners to withdraw certain amounts at certain times without penalty.

Insights

UNRELIABLE
COMPARISONS

Magazine articles and internet blogs that make comparisons are often misleading.

BETTER INTEREST
RATES

Annuities have consistently produced higher interest rates than CDs over longer periods.

COMPARABLE COSTS

Both annuities and CDs are purchased net of commissions and costs.

WITHDRAWAL PENALTIES

Both CDs and annuities have penalties for early withdrawals.

GUARANTEES

Insurance company guarantees are very strong, but not as strong as FDIC guarantees.

CHAPTER 3

————How Good Are Life Insurance Company ————
Guarantees?

Highlights
1. You should be concerned about the guarantees offered by the life insurance company that you are considering when purchasing a fixed or indexed annuity.

2. Life insurance companies have failed in the past, but those who purchased annuities almost always received their money back.

3. Only purchase annuities from companies that have at a minimum an A− rating from the top four rating companies, and a 75 or above rating from COMDEX.

4. Make sure your annuity professional shares all of the rating information with you. |

Insights

IMPORTANCE OF GUARANTEES	Poorly-rated insurance companies have failed.
IMPORTANCE OF HIGH RATINGS	Only purchase annuities from companies that have an A.M. Best minimum A- rating, and a COMDEX rating of at least 75.
STATE GUARANTEES	Your state has a guarantee fund that insures your principal. Check your coverage through your state insurance department.
CREDITOR PROTECTION	Annuities enjoy special privileges making them partially to totally immune from the claims of creditors, depending on each state's laws.

CHAPTER 4

—— **Do I Need Guaranteed Income Now? Later?** ——
For Others? Never?

Highlights

1. Knowing who you want to receive your annuity proceeds, and when those needs have to be met are essential factors in choosing the right annuity for you.

2. There are a number of annuity options, and each option is priced differently. Life insurance companies assess the risk and cost associated with each option to determine its price.

3. A fixed annuity has a guaranteed income amount; an indexed annuity is tied to stock market indexes, but still offers guaranteed amounts.

4. Surrender charges and income tax considerations may also affect the type of annuity or annuities that you choose.

Insights

INCOME NOW	SPIAs produce immediate income.
KNOWING WHAT FITS YOU	Knowing who you want to receive your annuity proceeds, and how and when they are to be received are decisions you will have to make with your annuity advisor.
ANNUITY OPTIONS	Insurance companies assess the risk and costs associated with each option, and price them differently.

CHAPTER 5

———— **How Your Money Grows inside Your** ————
Indexed Annuity

Highlights

1. Make sure that the company you select is trustworthy in terms of its guarantee to remain in business to protect the safety of your money. In our view this means that your advisor should recommend companies with an "A" in their rating.

2. Understand the limiting modifications companies impose on your earnings, regardless of what indexes you select or by what method earnings will be credited to your annuity. They are easily identified as the participation, cap, and spread rates.

3. Regardless of all of the choices available to you, the results attained by each of them will be just about the same over time.

4. An indexed annuity will likely earn 1 to 2 percent more than a fixed annuity, and most likely perform better than CDs based on documented history.

Insights

COMPANIES MAKE MONEY

Company actuaries make sure that they make money off of your money during the accumulation period, and thereafter if you die when or before the tables predict.

TIME VALUE OF MONEY

The longer you leave your money in the accumulation period, the more you will receive later.

LONGER ACCUMULATION PERIODS

The longer a company has your money to invest, the more money you will both make.

GREATER CURRENT INCOME

Historically, company-declared income has almost always been greater than its guaranteed income.

Insights, *cont'd*

LIMITED "INDEX" GAINS

Your annuity only gets a portion of the index gains based on your contract's participation, cap, and spread rates that limit your upside.

CREDITING INDEXED INCREASES

There are 42 different accounting crediting methods that companies offer—likely with more coming—that determine how much you will receive from index increases that all end in basically the same place.

NO LOSS ON INDEX LOSSES

Index losses do not create losses in your annuity.

MULTIPLE INDEXES

You can allocate your money among multiple indexes.

LONGER TERMS; BETTER RESULTS

Linking to longer index periods produces better results.

TOO MANY CHOICES

This is where the advice and counsel of your annuity advisor helps you to make the right decisions.

CHAPTER 6
Income Riders

Highlights

1. An income rider is a feature of an indexed annuity that provides additional income that is significantly in excess of an annuity's guaranteed rate.

2. Income riders allow you to keep control over your principal to a greater extent than SPIAs.

3. Your interest rate will never go lower than the rate you purchased in your income rider, but it could increase if your earnings in the base annuity outperform the interest rate in the income rider.

4. The insurance company does not actually fund the income rider amount; it tracks the account and the interest it makes using an accounting entry on its books.

5. There are limits on how much you can receive under your income rider that are set out in your contract.

6. Income riders, while very effective planning tools, are complex and offer a number of options; so it is important that you work with your advisor to determine if an income rider is right for you.

Insights

REMAIN SEPARATE

Income riders do not affect or control the terms of your base annuity contract and are not affected by it.

PAY HIGHER INTEREST RATES

Both advisors and clients focus on the higher interest rates paid by these riders (typically, from 4 to 12 percent)

COST

They cost from ¾ to 1 percent annually, charged against the value of your accumulation account.

COMMISSIONS

There aren't any.

SPIA CONVERSION

If you convert your annuity with an income rider to a SPIA, you will forfeit the build-up in your income account.

EXCLUSION RATIO

Income-for-life payments do not receive the exclusion ratio.

INCOME RIDERS AND DEATH

Most income riders stop at your death.

INCOME PAYMENTS

Companies limit your income payments based upon a payout schedule.

CHAPTER 7

———————————— **Long-Term-Care Riders** ————————————

Highlights

1. You can purchase a long-term-care rider that attaches to a fixed or indexed annuity or to purchase a hybrid annuity that includes LTC coverage.

2. The health underwriting standards for LTC riders are less stringent, relatively faster, and simpler than the underwriting standards for a traditional LTC policy.

3. Obtaining LTC coverage should not be your single reason for purchasing an annuity, but it can be an important factor in your decision-making process.

4. LTC rider distributions are first applied to your accumulated account value until it is exhausted, and thereafter from your insurance company.

5. LTC riders come with a cost, and should always be compared to a traditional LTC insurance policy by an LTC expert.

Insights

UNDERWRITING

Health underwriting standards for LTC riders are less stringent and relatively fast.

SECONDARY
CONSIDERATION

Obtaining LTC coverage should be a secondary reason for purchasing an annuity.

DISTRIBUTIONS

LTC distributions are first applied to your accumulated account value, and thereafter from the insurance company's money.

CHAPTER 8
Bonuses

Highlights

1. A bonus is a payment from an insurance company that adds money to your fixed or indexed annuity's base contract amount at the time of your purchase.

2. A bonus is a fixed percentage of your annuity premium and can be a one-time payment or multi-year payments.

3. Bonuses come with costs: Participation and cap rates are lower than with non-bonus annuities, and there may be additional surrender charges.

4. A common use for a bonus is when one annuity is exchanged for another. The bonus is used to fully or partially offset the surrender charge of the annuity that is being replaced.

5. It is extremely important for you and your annuity advisor to do the math to make sure that the bonus will prove to be profitable for you over time.

6. Always check the rating of the insurance company that is offering a bonus; the higher the bonus is, the more likely it is being sold by a lower-rated company.

Insights

PAY WELL	Companies add from 1 to 12 percent to your base contract's value the day it is created.
A "CAVEAT"	Highest bonuses are often offered by poorly rated companies.
COST	Companies do not charge for bonuses.
RECAPTURE CHARGES	Companies recapture a portion of their payments under bonus surrender charge tables if you terminate your contract early.
OFFSETTING SURRENDER CHARGES	Bonuses are helpful in offsetting the losses caused by surrender charges if you exchange contracts between different companies.
LIMITATIONS	Companies paying unusually large bonuses have significant limitations on participation, cap, or spread rates so that the company can still make its profits.

CHAPTER 9
─────────── The Taxation of Annuities ───────────

Highlights

1. The principal of an annuity—your premium(s)—is not subject to income tax when you make withdrawals; unless the annuity is held in an IRA, 401(k) plan, or a company-sponsored qualified retirement plan.

2. All withdrawals from your IRA are income-taxed as ordinary income.

3. Other than annuities with income riders and a few other minor exceptions, each annuity payment you receive is partly tax-free return of principal and partly taxable income because of the exclusion ratio.

4. You or your IRA can exchange one annuity for another tax free under section 1035 of the Internal Revenue Code.

5. Gifts of annuities, including irrevocable trusts, are subject to federal gift taxation, and cause immediate taxation of all of the annuity's earnings. If the gift is of an IRA-owned annuity, it will cause immediate income-taxation of all proceeds.

6. Annuities with a death benefit are included in the estates of their owners, and the beneficiaries will owe income taxes on any annuity earnings as received.

Insights

TAX DEFERRAL

Tax-free deferral is a major benefit of fixed and indexed annuities.

LIFO ACCOUNTING

"Last in First Out" accounting will always tax your distributions first as income, unless you annuitize your contract to utilize the exclusion ratio.

EXCLUSION RATIO

If you own the annuity when you annuitize your contract, part will be tax-free as a withdrawal of principal and part will be taxable income. If your IRA owns the annuity, it will not be able to use the exclusion ratio.

QUICK CALCULATION

You can divide the principal by the ending value to get an estimation of the percentage that will be tax-free under the exclusion ratio. Better yet, ask your insurance company for the exact calculation.

Insights, *cont'd*

TAX-FREE TRANSFERS

Internal Revenue Code Section 1035 allows you to transfer an annuity into other annuities without tax consequences.

PENALTY TAX

Withdrawals of income before age 59½ will pay 10 percent penalty tax on that income.

SURRENDER CHARGES

Surrender charges are not tax deductible.

LIVING TRUST AS BENEFICIARY

Your trustee will have to receive all distributions within five years.

INCOME TAX ON SURRENDER

You pay tax on what you receive, less your principal.

FEDERAL ESTATE TAX

The value of your annuity will be included in your estate for federal estate tax purposes.

FEDERAL GIFT TAX

A gift of your annuity is a taxable gift for federal gift tax purposes.

CHAPTER 10
——————— Commissions and Fees ———————

Highlights

1. There are no commissions or administrative and maintenance fees associated with fixed and indexed annuities that are paid directly by you.

2. All of an insurance company's costs in connection with building, distributing, and selling fixed and indexed annuities, along with the costs of administering and maintaining them, are taken into account when the insurance company prices the annuity.

3. Critics who attack the high costs and commissions associated with annuities either confuse or fail to adequately explain the differences between variable annuities—which do have high costs and commissions—and fixed and indexed annuities that do not have them.

4. Commissions are not built into or paid on income riders.

Insights

UNRELIABLE CRITICISMS

Do not believe articles criticizing commissions; they are incorrect.

NET-COST BASIS

You do not pay a commission or administrative or management charges when you purchase fixed or indexed annuities. Their costs are built into your contract on a net-cost basis to cover company costs.

CHAPTER 11

—— **Is a Fixed or Indexed Annuity Suitable for You?** ——

Highlights

1. You should only buy an annuity if it is suitable for you.

2. The burden of determining if an annuity is suitable for you is primarily on the advisor who sells the annuity to you, but we feel strongly that you have a responsibility to participate fully and honestly in the suitability discussions.

3. Suitability is based on a number of financial and personal factors that ensure that you have the need for an annuity as a part of your overall savings and retirement planning.

4. You should expend the time to make sure that you have a fundamental understanding of the basic features of the annuity that you intend to purchase and how it will benefit you.

Insights

RESPONSIBILITY OF
OTHERS

Insurance companies and annuity advisors are responsible for making sure that an annuity is suitable for you at the time of purchase.

YOUR RESPONSIBILITY

We believe you also need to take responsibility for determining whether or not a fixed or indexed annuity is suitable for you.

STATE INSURANCE
DEPARTMENTS

If you have a problem with either the company or your advisor, your state's insurance department will investigate and take action, if warranted, to save you the time, aggravation, and expense of doing so.

CHAPTER 12
——— The Alleged Benefits of Fixed Annuities ———

Highlights
1. Fixed annuities have not been subjected to the degree of criticism that has been levied against their indexed cousins.
2. There are a great many benefits and reasons for using fixed annuities that every advisor and potential annuity purchaser should be aware of.
3. Fixed annuities are not investments. They are long-term financial vehicles and should only be used for that purpose.
4. When used properly, fixed annuities can be an effective method to meet a person's financial goals.

Our Judgment

VALIDITY OF CLAIMS

Most all benefits claimed by advocates are factually accurate.

CHAPTER 13

——— The Alleged Detriments of Fixed Annuities ———

Highlights

1. Fixed annuities have been criticized for their lack of "investment" potential. Fixed annuities are not investments. They are long-term financial vehicles and should only be critiqued with that purpose in mind.

2. There are a great many allegations against their use, some of which every advisor and potential annuity purchaser should be aware of.

3. Most all of the allegations against them have been hollow or unsubstantiated.

4. When used properly, fixed annuities can be an effective method to meet a person's financial goals.

Our Judgment

VALIDITY OF CRITICISMS   Most all criticisms reflect bias and are not substantiated by the facts.

CHAPTER 14

——— The Alleged Benefits of Indexed Annuities ———

Highlights

1. Indexed annuities have been subject to a debate as to their effectiveness since their inception.

2. There are a great benefits and reasons for using indexed annuities that every advisor and potential annuity purchaser should be aware of.

3. Indexed annuities are not investments. They are long-term financial vehicles and should only be used for that purpose.

4. When used properly, indexed annuities can be an effective method to meet a person's financial goals.

Our Judgment

VALIDITY OF CLAIMS

Most all benefits claimed by advocates are factually accurate.

CHAPTER 15
——The Alleged Detriments of Indexed Annuities ——

Highlights

1. Indexed annuities have been subject to a debate as to their "investment" effectiveness. Indexed annuities are not investments. They are long-term financial vehicles and should only be critiqued with that purpose in mind.

2. There are a many allegations against their use, some of which every advisor and potential annuity purchaser should be aware of.

3. Most of the allegations against them have been hollow or unsubstantiated.

4. When used properly, indexed annuities can be an effective method to meet a person's financial goals.

Our Judgment

VALIDITY OF CRITICISMS   Most all criticisms reflect bias and are not substantiated by the facts.

The Masters Institute Fellows

Mark Billes, President
Safe and Secure Retirement and
Insurance Services, Inc.
17011 Beach Blvd., Suite 900
Huntington Beach, CA 92647
714-791-3084
msbilles@hotmail.com

Stephen J. Buchanan, B.A., J.D.
Weson
The Fulton House
4555 Fulton Avenue, Suite 210
Sherman Oaks, CA 91423
213-305-9891
sjbweson@gmail.com

Dan Campana, President
Lifecor Insurance Solutions
2059 Camden Avenue, Suite 122
San Jose, CA 95124
408-531-0500
campanad@yahoo.com

Tom Chapman, LUTCF,
President
Chapman Wealth Strategies
Insurance & Financial Solutions
1432 Edinger Avenue, Suite 130
Tustin, CA 92780
949-891-6745
tom@chapmanwealthstrategies.com

Richard Chinnery
117 N. 17th Street
Lexington, MO 64063
660-269-2830
customplanners@gmail.com

Dan Cooper, LUTCF, CAS, RFC,
President
Blueprint Advisory Group
4024 Oleander Drive, Suite A-1
Wilmington, NC 28403
910-790-7990 Fax: 910-790-9018
dancooper@
blueprintretirement.com

John P. Dubots, President
Dubots Capital Management, LLC
27710 Jefferson Avenue, Suite 101
Temecula, CA 92590
951-699-1502
jdubots@
jpdcapitalmanagement.com

Rob Esperti, President
Surfers Insurance, Inc.
2381 Newport Avenue
Cardiff by the Sea, CA 92007
760-473-7490
rob@surfersinsurance.com

Travis Evans, President
Evans Financial Group
511 University Drive East
College Station, TX 77840
979-846-3570
travis@evansfg.com

Dave Ficarra, President
Ficarra Accounting and Tax
34450 Coachwood
Sterling Heights, MI 48312
586-978-7963
dave@quartermasterwealth.com

Graydon Garner, CFP,
Managing Partner
Colburn Advisors LLC
200 Pemberwick Road
Greenwich, CT 06831
Office: 203-487-0144
Cell: 203-524-5921
graydon@graygarner.com

Dana D. Gibson, President
Prime Retirement And Income
Solutions
3312 Dunbar Avenue
Fort Collins, CO 80526
970-460-6835
bettersolutions911@gmail.com

David Gollner, President & CEO
Legacy Financial Strategies, Inc.
3087 Innovation Way
Hermitage, PA 16148
724-983-1617
david@leavealegacy.com

Dick M. Griffis, RFC, President
Griffis Wealth Management
208 Peterson Avenue, S., Suite 206
Douglas, GA 31533
912-384-4545 Fax: 877-610-2829
dgriffis@
southgeorgiafinancialservices.com

Ronald J. Harvey, J.D., President
Harvey and Companies, Inc.
2950 5th Avenue North
St. Petersburg, FL 33713
727-867-1000 Fax: 727-867-2786
ronharvey@
harveyandcompanies.com

Patrick A. Jeffers,
Executive Director
The Masters Institute - TMI III, Inc.
28858 N. 95th Way
Scottsdale, AZ 85262
800-476-8682 Fax: 602-865-1931
patrick@themastersinstitute.us

Stewart Spencer King, CLU,
CHFC
DownEast Financial
287 Meekins Road
Bayboro, NC, 28515
Phone/Fax: 252-745-1203
Cell: 252-670-4616
1979tr7@gmail.com

Rock R. La Spada, President
Diamond Sage Financial, LLC
3675 Rainbow Blvd., Suite 107-111
Las Vegas, NV 89103
702-277-2730
indigobluesixty@aol.com

David E. LaBounty
Strategic Insurance, Inc.
2141 E. Broadway Road, Suite 220
Tempe, AZ 85282
480-779-4421 Fax: 480-967-1152
dave@strategicinsurance.com

Gertrudis Martinez, President
TC Insurance Services, Inc.
1650 Margaret Street, Suite
302-107
Jacksonville, FL 32204
904-556-6388
tulie.martinez@gmail.com

Barry Munro, President
Munro Legacy Planners LLC
321 Creekstone Ridge
Woodstock, GA 30188
Phone: 770-321-6648
Fax: 770-216-1843
barry@Mlplanners.com

Dennis S. Parks, President
Senior Estate Planners, LLC
1701 S. Flagler Drive, Suite 404
West Palm Beach, FL 33401
561-568-4723
parktota@gmail.com

G. L. Phelps, President
South Texas Estate Planning
Services, LLC
14310 Northbrook Drive, Suite 100
San Antonio, TX 78232
210-499-5392
LinPhelps@sbcglobal.net

Drew Popelka, CPA, President
Popelka Law Firm PLLC
3000 South 31st Street, Suite 303
Temple, TX 76502
254-774-7880
templeattorney@sbcglobal.net

Don Rasmussen, AIF, CFEd,
CAP, President
Quartermaster Wealth Management
124 Floyd Smith Blvd., Suite 325
Charlotte, NC 28262
704-490-4111
don@quartermasterwealth.com

Laine Schoneberger, CLU,
ChFC, President
Strategic Insurance, Inc.
2141 E. Broadway Road, Suite 220
Tempe, AZ 85282
480-779-4421 Fax: 480-967-1152
laine@strategicinsurance.com

Jeffrey P. Schwebach, President
Schwebach Financial
505 East 4th Street
PO Box 69
Dell Rapids, SD 57022
605-428-4275 Fax: 605-428-4692
lschway@gmail.com

Doug Scott, President
Cromarty Consultants LLC
1250 Bethlehem Pike, Suite 104
Hatfield, PA 19440
267-253-0129
d1scott@comcast.net

David R. Smith, President
DRS Advisory Services
2173 Salk Avenue, Suite 250
Carlsbad, CA 92008
877-842-2676
acorn4u@sbcglobal.net

Jerry G. Sutton, President
Sutton Advisors, PLC
2201 East Grand River Avenue
Lansing, MI 48912
517-487-5555 Fax: 517-487-5770
jerry@suttonadvisors.com

Bernard A. Unger,
Chartered Advisor in Philanthropy
Buffalo Financial Group, LLC
2875 Union Road, Suite 351
Cheektowaga, NY 14227
716-698-8928
bufplanner@cs.com

Heath Walters, CPA, President
Walters CPA and SAFE College
Funding
6047 Tyvola Glen Circle
Charlotte, NC 28217
704-708-9949
heath@walterscpagroup.com

· NOTES ·

1 "Annuity Holders Need Not Fear Carrier Failure," Marrion, Jack (Senior Market Advisor, June 1, 2009)

2 "How Safe are Annuities?", Tomlinson, Joe (*Advisor Perspective, Inc.*, August 14, 2012)

3 Internet Blog; Glenn Daily, www.Advisors4Advisors.com, July 22, 2009.

4 "Indexed Annuities – Interest Crediting," Sheryl Moore (http://www.retirementthinktank.com/indexed-annuities-interest-crediting/ , March 23, 2012)

5 "Indexed Annuities are a Safety Trap," Gibbs, Lisa (*Money* magazine: Investor's Guide, January 17, 2011)

6 NAFA response to Money magazine article, O'Brien, Kim, http://www.consolpro.com/uploads/NAFA_Responds_to_Money_Mag.pdf

7 IBID

8 Real World Index Annuity Returns, Jack Marrion, Geoffrey VanderPal, David F. Babbel, revised Version, December 27, 2010 Wharton Financial Institutions Center, P

9 *Annuities for Dummies*, Pechter, Kerry, (Wiley Publishing, 2008)

accumulation period. The period before annuitization when an annuity owner holds assets in a tax-deferred manner.

age at annuitization. Age of the annuitant when an annuity contract is annuitized.

annual reset crediting method. A crediting method for index-linked interest that is determined each year by comparing the index value at the end of the contract year with the index value at the start of that contract year, and giving interest credit for the difference, if it is greater.

annuitant. A person who buys or creates an annuity, and whose life expectancy is used to determine payments.

annuitization. The time at which an annuity is converted into a stream of regular payments, either for the lifetime of the annuitant or the lifetimes of the annuitant and the joint annuitant.

annuitization period. The period of the policy when the amount built-up or accumulated during the accumulation phase is paid out to the annuitant in the form of systematic payments.

annuitize. To begin a series of payments from an annuity.

annuity. A contract sold by a life insurance company that provides fixed or variable payments to an annuitant, either immediately or at a future date, usually to supplement retirement income.

annuity owner. The person or people who have the rights to make withdrawals from the annuity, surrender or change the designated beneficiary, and make decisions over all of the other annuity terms.

application. A form that must be completed by an individual who is purchasing an annuity.

back end load. A charge that is incurred when money is withdrawn from a contract, through loan or surrender.

bail-out provision. An option that permits an annuitant to withdraw money without penalty if the rate of return drops by a certain amount from the initially guaranteed rate.

basic features. Annuity contract provisions such as surrender charges, guaranteed interest rates, bonus interest rates, indexed rate crediting methods, tax-deferred growth, lifetime income riders, annuitization options, nursing home benefits, and other living or death benefits.

beneficiary. The person who receives the balance of an annuity after the death of a payee.

bonus. The additional interest paid by a life insurance company that is typically used as an incentive for a purchaser to choose its annuity policy over another and to offset the surrender charge when a new annuity is exchanged for an old one with a different company.

cap rate. A company imposed limit on the amount of interest an indexed annuity can earn during the term chosen by the annuitant. For example, assume the chosen index is up 10 percent over the term, and the contract has an 8 percent cap rate. The annuity would only be credited with 8 percent. See also **index term.**

carrier. The underwriting insurance company.

certificate of deposit (CD). Short or medium-term, interest-bearing, FDIC-insured debt instrument offered by banks and savings and loans. A low risk investment vehicle with low returns and early withdrawal penalty.

claw-back. A feature sometimes found in an annuity contract that provides that if a withdrawal of more than the 10 percent

penalty-free amount is taken, the life
retroactively charges a surrender fee on all pr..

COMDEX. A composite index that averages th..
four primary rating services into a single score from.
100 being the highest rating.

commercial annuity. A contract between you and
insurance company, where you give the company mone,
usually in a lump sum—in exchange for the company's promi..
to give it back to you over a period of time with added interest or,
in some cases, appreciation in the value of the principal.

contract anniversary. The anniversary of the annuity
contract issuance date.

contract year. A twelve-month period commencing with
the annuity contract issuance date and with each contract
anniversary thereafter. See also **crediting date.**

cost basis. The after-tax premiums paid to an annuity that
is not owned by a retirement plan. Since these amounts were
previously taxed, the cost basis is not taxable when withdrawn.
See also **exclusion ratio.**

cost of living adjustment (COLA). A method used to adjust
an annuity's payout to reflect increases in the consumer price
index or other measure of inflation.

crediting date. The date at the end of a crediting period when
interest earnings are credited to an indexed annuity. this can be
a once per year anniversary date, every other year biennial date,
and we have also seen crediting dates every three, four, five, and
even ten years.

crediting methods. Ways in which the increases in the value
of the selected indexes are credited to an indexed annuity.

current interest rate. The interest rate that an annuity is
paying, including the sum of the base rate, if any and the bonus
rate, if any. The current rate is set by the insurance company at
the time of issuance and is guaranteed for a specific length of
time.

ath benefit. The payment the annuitant's beneficiaries will eceive.

deferred annuity. An "accumulation" annuity product under which payments are made by the annuitant (either through a single premium or a series of periodic payments) and left to accumulate on a tax-deferred basis over a period of years.

declared rate. The interest rate a company will pay on the anniversary of each annuity if rates are higher than the guaranteed rate. The declared rate is not contractual, but has always been paid if greater than the guaranteed rate.

early termination penalty. See **surrender charge.**

end-of-term date. See **crediting date.**

equity-indexed annuity. An annuity whose returns are based upon the performance of an equity market index, such as the S&P 500, DJIA, or NASDAQ. The principal investment is protected from losses in the equity market, while gains add to the annuity's returns.

exclusion ratio. The ratio that determines which portion of an annuity distribution is earnings and which portion is a return of capital. Only the portion consisting of earnings is taxable.

Federal Deposit Insurance Corporation (FDIC). An independent agency of the federal government that insures deposits in banks and thrift institutions for at least $250,000.

Financial Industry Regulatory Authority (FINRA). A regulatory body over securities advisors.

fixed annuity. A deferred accumulation vehicle offered by insurance companies that guarantees a stream of fixed payments during the life of the annuitant.

fixed payout option. A payment option providing for payments which remain fixed throughout the payment period and do not vary with the investment performance of the annuity's underlying funds.

fixed bucket. An annuity option that allows the allocation of a percentage of an indexed annuity to a one-year fixed guaranteed rate.

fixed guarantee period. A set period of time for a guarantee.

fixed payment plan. An annuity plan payout option that distributes payments in set amounts. Fixed plans provide for the systematic liquidation of principal and interest in a series of equal periodic payments that do not fluctuate over time.

free-look period. A period, usually within the first thirty days of receiving your annuity contract, when you may opt out of an annuity contract and receive all of your money back.

guaranteed minimum accumulation benefit. A guarantee that the account value will be a certain amount at a certain point in the future.

high-water mark. A crediting method for index-linked interest that is determined by looking at the index's value at various points during the term, and is based on the difference between its highest value during the term and the index value at the beginning of the term.

hybrid annuity. Generic name used to describe many types of fixed and indexed annuities offering one or more riders. See also long-term-care-rider and income rider.

imaginary account. See **income account.**

immediate annuity. An annuity product under which payments begin within thirty days following premium payment.

income account. Also known as an imaginary account, it is an account that is part of an income rider and does not contain actual funds. The company simply makes an accounting entry that reflects the income benefit base plus the interest rate that the income rider guarantees.

income benefit base. The income account value used in an income rider upon which lifetime income payments are calculated: Your premium plus the roll-up rate added annually, less any withdrawals taken. It cannot be withdrawn other than by taking guaranteed lifetime income payments.

income rider. An added feature of an indexed annuity that provides an optional lifetime income stream from a stated income base amount which grows each year at a rate in excess of an annuity's guaranteed rate.

indexed annuity. A deferred savings vehicle offered by insurance companies that guarantees a minimum interest rate while offering the opportunity for a higher interest rate by linking with a stock index. No matter what happens to the index, the annuity will never earn less than the guaranteed rate.

index interest. Used with an indexed annuity, that percentage of the index's increase in value that is added to the annuity at the end of a selected time period.

index term. The period of time over which a selected index is measured. Typically, it is monthly, annually, or over a period of two or more years.

individual retirement account (IRA) A traditional form of retirement account authorized under the Internal Revenue Code.

inflation-indexed annuity. An annuity with a rider that contains a cost-of-living adjustment so that the payments track with inflation.

joint annuity. A type of annuity payment option that guarantees a lifetime income for two or more persons; mostly used by spouses.

leveraging factors. An option for a long-term-care rider that provides a multiple of an annuity's accumulation value, ranging from 150 to 300 percent, as an additional long term care benefit.

life-only annuity. An annuity in which payments are guaranteed to be paid at regular intervals for the life of the annuitant. Also known as a life-income annuity.

life annuity plus a period certain. A life annuity that guarantees payments will continue for a specified number of years. If the annuitant dies before the period certain has expired, payments will be made to a beneficiary for the duration of the period certain.

life income plus a period certain. An annuity that pays income for the life of the annuitant plus a stated period.

last in, first out (LIFO). A form of taxation of an annuity (typically one with an income rider) that taxes the earnings first and the principal thereafter. The earnings are considered to be the last amounts credited to the annuity and the premiums the first.

long-term-care rider. An annuity option that pays a tax-free benefit if the annuitant qualifies for long term care. Sometimes called a hybrid annuity.

low-water mark. An interest crediting method that uses the lowest point of the index value during the measurement period.

multi-year bonus. A type of bonus that is paid over a number of years rather than immediately upon the purchase of an annuity. See also **bonuses.**

National Association of Insurance Commissioners (NAIC). The national system of state-based insurance regulation in the United States. It was created and is governed by the chief insurance regulators from the fifty states, the District of Columbia and five U.S. Territories.

National Association for Fixed Annuities (NAFA). A lobbying association whose purpose is to educate regulators, legislators, consumers, members of the media, industry personnel, and distributors about fixed annuities (including indexed annuities) and their benefits to retirees and those planning for retirement.

no-surrender annuity. An annuity that does not have a surrender charge.

non-forfeiture rate. The minimum interest rate that an insurance company can use in an individual fixed annuity contract to determine its cash value. This rate is set by each state.

nonqualified deferred annuity. A contract that provides for tax deferral of investment income until withdrawn from the contract. Fixed annuities offer a fixed rate of return for a stipulated period, while variable annuities offer investment options.

nonqualified income annuity. A contract that provides periodic payments based on life or joint-life expectancies plus a period certain (i.e., life plus ten years certain). The periodic payment amount is based on the amount used to purchase the contract, the terms of the payout, and an assumed rate of return.

partial surrender. An amount taken from an annuity that exceeds the penalty-free withdrawal amount. It is subject to a surrender charge.

participation rate. A method by which a life insurance company limits the interest credited to an indexed annuity based upon a percentage of the overall increase in the index. for example, if the calculated change in the index is 10 percent and the participation rate is 70 percent, the index-linked interest rate for your annuity will be 7 percent ($10\% \times 70\% = 7\%$)

payee. The person who receives periodic payments from an annuity. This is usually also the owner of the contract and the same person who is the annuitant. See also **beneficiary.**

penalty-free withdrawals. Any withdrawal from an annuity that is not subject to a surrender charge.

period certain. The payout option on an annuity that guarantees installment income for a specific number of years, e.g. ten or twenty years. If the annuitant dies during this specified time period, the beneficiary will receive the remaining payments.

point-to-point crediting method. An index-linked interest crediting method that is based on the *difference* between the index's value at the end of the selected term and the index's value at the start of that term.

private annuity. A personal or restricted annuity. The major difference between private annuities and commercial annuities is that the person or entity that assumes the obligation for the private annuity is not in the business of selling annuities. Used primarily for estate planning.

qualified annuities. Annuities purchased for funding an IRA, 403(b) tax-deferred annuity, or other type of retirement arrangements.

rating agencies. Agencies who periodically rate the strength of life insurance companies. The "big four" in the rating business are: A.M. Best, Fitch; Moody's, and Standard and Poor's. A fifth rating company, COMDEX, rates life insurance companies on the average percentile of a company's ratings from the four others.

recapture charges. A separate surrender charge that may apply to bonuses if an annuity is surrendered early or if withdrawals exceed the free withdrawal amount.

risk tolerance. The degree of uncertainty that an investor is willing to tolerate when choosing an investment. Those who have low-risk tolerance invest in assets that are safer and less likely to result in a loss.

roll-up rate. The interest rate that an income rider provides in determining the annual increase to the benefit base.

safety-first rule. The tenet that the preservation of principal is more important than increasing the level of risk to increase possible upside returns.

single-premium immediate annuity (SPIA). A fixed, immediate annuity that is purchased with a single lump sum premium, providing payments for life or for a specified period commencing immediately at the next payment period following issuance of the annuity contract.

split annuity. Combines a single-premium, deferred annuity and a single-premium, immediate annuity.

spread. A company-imposed limit on the interest an indexed annuity can receive that is computed by subtracting a specific percentage from any change in the index. for example, if a contract has a 2 percent spread and the index increases 10 percent, the annuity would be credited with 8 percent (10% minus the spread of 2% = 8%).

suitability. The determination by and annuity advisor that there is a "reasonable basis" to believe that an individual understands an annuity's basic features and that the annuity is appropriate for that person.

suitability information. The information that the National Association of Insurance Commissioners (NAIC) requires annuity advisors to obtain to determine if an annuity is appropriate (suitable) for a person who is considering the purchase of an annuity.

surrender charge. The fee assessed by a life insurance company upon the early cancellation of an annuity. Also called an early termination penalty or withdrawal charge.

systematic withdrawals. A feature of many annuity contracts that avoids surrender charges on withdrawals provided they are taken in equal payments over at least five years. Systematic withdrawals avoid the 10 percent tax penalty if the annuitant is under 59½ years of age.

tax-free exchange. The exchange of one insurance or annuity contract for another. It is also known as a section 1035 exchange because of the Internal Revenue Code provision that defines the rules for tax-free exchanges of insurance and annuity contracts.

term-certain annuity. An annuity with income payments over a set number of years.

time horizon. The length of time an annuity must stay in force until the annuitant can receive a distribution without surrender charges.

variable annuity. An investment annuity that risks principal by market gains and losses and that is not covered in this book. It may only be sold by individuals who, in addition to being licensed life insurance agents, are registered representatives.

waivers. Options in annuities that waive surrender charges when the annuitant requires nursing home care, has a terminal illness, or suffers a disability.

withdrawal charge. See **surrender charge.**

withdrawal table. A contract provision in an income rider that limits how much income base can be withdrawn annuallly.